GUERRILLA PRIEST

AN AMERICAN FAMILY
IN WORLD WAR II PHILIPPINES

GUERRILLA PRIEST

AN AMERICAN FAMILY
IN WORLD WAR II PHILIPPINES

STEPHEN GRIFFITHS

DANCING MOON PRESS
NEWPORT, OREGON

GUERRILLA PRIEST
AN AMERICAN FAMILY IN WORLD WAR II PHILIPPINES
COPYRIGHT © STEPHEN GRIFFITHS, 2016
ALL RIGHTS RESERVED

Paperback ISBN: 978-1-937493-93-6
Ebook ISBN: 978-1-937493-94-3
Library of Congress Control Number: 2016937889

Griffiths, Stephen
Guerrilla Priest: An American Family in World War II Philippines
1. Philippines-World War II; 2. Philippines-Guerrilla Resistance World War II; 3. Philippines-Japanese Prisoner of War camps; 4. Philippines-Balbalasang, Kalinga-Apayao; 5. Philippines-Tingguian people; 6. Philippines-Philippine Episcopal Church. I. TITLE

Book editing, design & production: *Carla Perry, Dancing Moon Press*
Cover design & production: *Sarah Gayle, Sarah Gayle Art*
Front cover portrait of Al Griffiths from a black & white photograph taken in Balbalasang in the 1930s: A.B. Duschane (1963)
Back cover photos from top to bottom: Saltan River valley and rice fields; Steve and Katy Griffiths, circa 1949; Saltan River, Balbalasang; Balbalasang villager; St. Paul's Church in Balbalasang. All photos by Al Griffiths.
Interior photos: most by Al Griffiths (otherwise photographer unknown)
Manufactured in the United States of America

DANCING MOON PRESS
P.O. Box 832, Newport, OR 97365
541-574-7708
www.dancingmoonpress.com
info@dancingmoonpress.com

FIRST EDITION

For my sister, Katy

And the villagers of
Balbalasang, Kalinga-Apayao,
Philippines

CONTENTS

Rev. Alfred L. Griffiths, circa early 1930s.

FROM BATTLE AND MURDER,
AND FROM SUDDEN DEATH,
GOOD LORD, DELIVER US.

—THE 1928 BOOK OF COMMON PRAYER

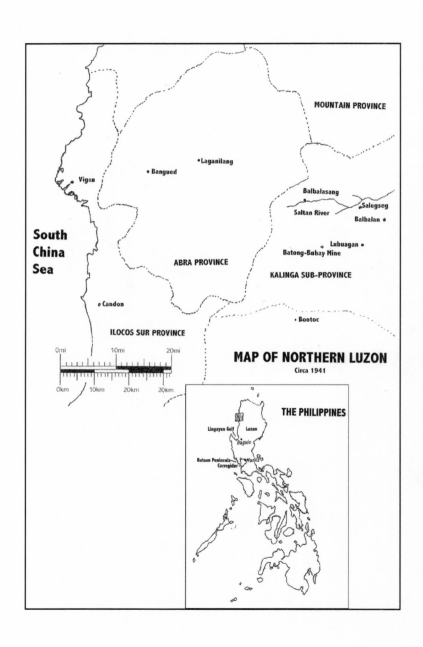

MOUNTAIN PROVINCE

•Laganilang

•Bangued

•Vigan

Balbalasang
Salegseg
Saltan River
Balbalan •

South
China
Sea

Lubuagan •
Batong-Buhay Mine

ABRA PROVINCE

KALINGA SUB-PROVINCE

•Candon

• Bontoc

ILOCOS SUR PROVINCE

0mi   10mi   20mi

0km   10km   20km   30km

MAP OF NORTHERN LUZON
Circa 1941

THE PHILIPPINES

Lingayen Gulf   Luzon
Baguio

Bataan Peninsula
Corregidor
Manila

Prologue

"I HID OUT IN THE MOUNTAINS OF LUZON for 16 months with my wife and child. When the Japanese captured me, I was tied to a bed for two weeks. The Japanese officer said he was going to kill me. He gave me a shovel. I thought I was going to dig my grave, but it turned out to be a Japanese trench. After digging trenches for two days, I was sent down to the Baguio concentration camp—Camp Holmes— and then to Bilibid here in Manila. It was a tough old life, but I have no regrets. But it sure is good to see the old Yanks again, believe me!"

On the U.S. Army Intelligence film, my father's voice is strong, and he speaks with no hesitation. It is February 1945, and he has just been liberated from a Japanese prisoner of war camp in the Philippines. The camera captures him waist up. Standing under a tree by a sun-drenched wall, he is thinner and younger than I have ever seen him. His hair is long and wavy. He is wearing a short-sleeved cotton shirt that is too big for him. His smile is bright and his face expressive. Mortar guns boom in the distance. The 37th Infantry is still fighting for possession of Manila, the capital city. He speaks in a Boston accent I'd forgotten he had.

My father's interview is the final one on a 90-minute film titled, *Death, Escape & Liberation: POWS in the Philippines During World War II.*[1] I didn't know it existed until recently, when an acquaintance brought it to my attention. My father, Rev. Alfred L. Griffiths—an Episcopal priest—never told me the story he relates on camera to Army Intelligence. Only when he was with friends who had been in prison camp with him did he—or my mother—ever talk about their wartime experiences. Instead, they each wrote an account of the war for my sister and me to have. The narrative of this book was derived from their two unpublished memoirs. They are truly more the authors of it than I am.

When I began editing and rewriting my parents' manuscripts, I was much older than they were when they lived through the experiences. I was constantly amazed— and sometimes very moved—by how they coped with their extraordinary circumstances. This project has reintroduced me to my parents and given me a new affection and respect for them and for other civilians caught up in the great changes that wartime demands.

---

[1] *Traditions Military Videos, DVD, 2005.*

A WHIRLWIND COURTSHIP

AL GRIFFITHS, A NATIVE OF MASSACHUSETTS and fresh out of Virginia Theological Seminary, first went to the Philippines in 1931 to become the chaplain of Brent School in Baguio. An Episcopal Church school, Brent served the sons and daughters of American colonial officials, missionaries, miners, and entrepreneurs.

The son of a Welsh immigrant, Al grew up in Methuen, Massachusetts, the only one of his four siblings to attend college. He chose Hobart College in western New York, and his parish rector, Rev. Malcolm Peabody, wrote him a glowing letter of recommendation: "Al Griffiths is a perfectly corking fellow who will benefit immensely from college training. I believe he will be very popular among the students and satisfactory to the faculty... I can only assure you he is clear gold all through."

Al joined a fraternity, signed up for Reserved Officer Training Corps (ROTC), ran cross-country, and took part in theatrical productions. He graduated in 1928 and entered Virginia Theological Seminary the following year, earning a Bachelor of Divinity in 1931. Eager to become acquainted with the Episcopal Church's mission work in northern Luzon, Al traveled throughout the Mountain Province during school vacations. He was especially enchanted by Balbalasang in the sub-province of Kalinga. On the upper reaches of the Saltan River and surrounded on all sides by pine-forested mountains like an amphitheater, the village was home to the Episcopal Church's most isolated mission, reached by a three-day hike from Laganilang in Abra Province to the west, or a two-day hike from Lubuagan in the mountainous interior.

Balbalasang villagers were famous throughout the region for their skill in crafting machetes, spears, and head axes. Numbering about thirty thousand, the Tingguians inhabited the sky land of Abra Province and the headwaters of the Saltan River in Kalinga. Their chief crop was rice, grown in irrigated terraces and in gardens cut from the forest, which were also planted to a wide variety of vegetables. When the gardens declined in productivity, they were abandoned and reverted to forest. The forest itself was rich in game—deer and wild pig, which the Tingguian hunted with spears.

The leader of the Balbalasang people was Chief Puyao. He had been appointed mayor of the Balbalan District in Kalinga shortly after the Spanish-American War. Respected and loved by his people, Chief Puyao had encouraged villagers to build an elementary school and teachers' quarters with wood they cut and carefully hewed from the forest. American colonial authorities were so impressed by his initiative that they assigned a supervising teacher and four assistants to the school.[2] Exploring the advantages to

---

[2] Fry, Howard T., *A History of the Mountain Province*, p. 161.

be gained by an even closer association with Americans, Chief Puyao invited the Episcopal Church to establish a mission in Balbalasang. The first missionary arrived in 1925.

The Tingguian, like other mountain tribes in northern Luzon known collectively as Igorots, had maintained their independence throughout three hundred years of Spanish colonial rule, never becoming acculturated like their lowland brethren. In contrast, the Americans and the Igorots quickly took to each other. Americans admired the Igorots' bravery and independent streak, and Igorots saw the advantages in education and health care by forming close associations with the new colonialists.

Not long after the United States acquired the Philippines from Spain in 1898, the Secretary of the Interior for the Philippines, Dean C. Worcester, visited Balbalasang on a tour of northern Luzon. In his account of his 1905 journey, he wrote:

> We visited several of the wilder settlements of the Tingians in Abra, then made a hard climb over Mount Pico de Loro and descended its eastern slopes to the Tingian village of Balbalasan in the Saltan River valley. Its people, while not really headhunters, were often obliged to defend themselves against their Kalinga neighbors, and were consequently well armed. [3]

The Kalinga had reputations as fierce headhunters. Whether motivated by revenge or youthful aspiration, the

---

[3] Worcester, Dean C., *The Philippines Past and Present*, Volume II, p. 538.

taking of an enemy's head was always a time of great rejoicing. However, peace pacts between villages served to reduce the incidence of headhunting, and the advent of American colonial rule gradually brought an end to headhunting as a cultural institution.

In 1936, the priest-in-charge of St. Paul's Mission in Balbalasang resigned. When Al heard the news, he asked the Episcopal Bishop of the Philippines for the assignment. At that time, he was serving as Chaplain of St. George's School in Rhode Island and missed the Philippines. He was eager to return to the Islands in a new role as a missionary rather than as a school chaplain. The Bishop quickly assented.

By 1936, St. Paul's Mission had grown to include a small church and several outstations, a dispensary, a girls' dormitory for students from neighboring villages who attended the elementary school, and two residences for mission staff. The buildings were made of pine and had thatched roofs. Dottie Taverner, a plump and cheerful British nurse in her fifties, staffed the dispensary.

Balbalasang villagers called their new priest *"Padji"* (father). His mission house stood on a hill above the church and plaza. He had a grand view of the Saltan River valley and the village below, almost hidden by coffee and tangerine trees. On both sides of the pine-forested valley, villagers had carved rice terraces fed by water drawn from mountain streams. At planting, the fields were a rich, muddy gray. They quickly turned bright green with seedlings and matured to a warm golden brown at harvest.

Flowing through sun-washed granite boulders, the Saltan River rushed past the village. Al swam in it almost every day. He wrote his friends in Massachusetts that the river was as fresh, clear, and sparkling as champagne.

One evening in the summer of 1937—after he had been in Balbalasang almost a year—Al turned on his short-wave radio to listen to the news. He was surprised to learn the Japanese had attacked Shanghai and that all American women and children there were being evacuated by ship to Manila. Wondering if a woman he had met at a church conference the year before—and who taught in Shanghai—might be among the refugees, Al made the long trek out of Balbalasang, caught a bus to Manila, and was dockside when the ship pulled in. Yes, Carey Coles was on board, but he did not know that she had just gotten married. The women in her wedding party were with her, including her unmarried sister, Nessie, a teacher in Hawaii.

Al and Nessie quickly struck up a friendship and for the next nine evenings in a row, they dined and danced—at the grand Manila Hotel, the Army-Navy Club, and the huge Santa Ana dance hall. They made a striking couple. Thin and tall as Al, Nessie had wavy black hair and pale, white skin. She wore no jewelry; her only make-up was lipstick. Al's curly blond hair had turned gray at the temples, but he was trim and tanned from his swimming and mountain hiking. He smiled often, making his green eyes sparkle.

Al Griffiths astride horse on the trail to Balbalasang,
circa 1930s.

After this whirlwind courtship, Nessie sailed back to Hawaii to begin the school year at St. Andrew's Priory in Honolulu, and Al returned to Balbalasang, a little less lonely. The two struck up a correspondence. But Nessie's teaching year in Honolulu was cut short when her father wrote from Oregon that her mother was very ill and not expected to live. Nessie sailed for Portland as soon as she could. When her mother died, her father bought three burial plots, one for his wife, one for himself and, Nessie assumed, the third for her—at thirty years of age the only one of his three daughters not to have married. When Al wrote a few weeks later to express his sympathy—and to ask her to marry him—she accepted immediately.

They decided to be married in November at St. John's Pro-cathedral in Shanghai so Carey could be her maid of honor and her brother-in-law, Charles, serve as Al's best man.

Sailing to Shanghai on the *Empress of Japan*, Nessie found herself one morning seated on a deck chair between two prominent missionaries, a Baptist and a Presbyterian, both on their way to Madras, India, to attend a church conference. The fact that Nessie was on her way to Shanghai came to the fore in the conversation.

"Yes," she said, "I'm to be married to a young clergyman stationed in the Philippines."

"How fine! What seminary did he graduate from?" inquired the Baptist.

Nessie swallowed not once, but twice before answering that she did not know.

The Baptist rose from his deck chair, offered a hand to assist Nessie in rising, and said, "Miss Coles, I think we should take a walk around the deck."

In the course of the next half-hour, he questioned Nessie further. Perhaps the only fact he did not learn was that Nessie didn't even know Al's full first name—whether it was Albert, Alfred, or Aloysius. The Baptist hesitated before he asked his final question, one that Nessie knew was surely coming.

"How long have you known your fiancé?"

Nessie had done enough swallowing. She answered quickly this time: "Nine days."

The Baptist's voice rose precipitously, "Miss Coles, do you realize what you are doing?"

Nessie mustered her courage and said, "Al lives in the most remote mission station in the Philippines. Six months from now I will either hate him or love him a great deal."

"Are you willing to take that chance?"

"Yes."

Then the Baptist rendered his surprising verdict: "Go right ahead."

On their wedding day, the front steps of the Pro-cathedral were banked with golden chrysanthemum, and the chancel with white ones. After a quick reception in the guildhall, Al and Nessie changed their clothes, grabbed their suitcases, and made off in a taxi for the ship that would take them to Hong Kong for their honeymoon. Shortly after the ship sailed, they heard a knock on their cabin door. Al opened the door to find the purser checking the passenger list. He asked Al what Nessie's name was.

"Ernestine Elizabeth," he said. "No wait...Elizabeth Ernestine?"

In frustration, he turned to Nessie and said, "What *is* your name, anyway?"

Nessie laughed, "It's Elizabeth Ernestine—and aren't you glad you're not wearing your clerical collar?"

After they disembarked at Hong Kong, Al discovered that he had packed one of the bed sheets along with his pajamas. And that he was missing his film. He and Nessie went to the shipping office to return the sheet and ask permission to go aboard and get the film. The film was nowhere to be found (Al found it later in his coat pocket), but he did spot his best pair of shoes, which he hadn't yet missed. At this point, Nessie was beginning to get a glimmer of what their life together would be like.

**Al and Nessie Griffiths on their wedding day,
November 12, 1938, St. John's Pro-Cathedral, Shanghai, China.**

MR. AND MRS. *PADJI*

WHEN THEY ARRIVED IN MANILA after their honeymoon, Al wired Dottie Taverner, asking her to arrange for *cargadores* (porters) to meet them at the trailhead in Abra Province. Nestled in the Cordillera Central at 2,800 feet, Balbalasang was 80 kilometers away—a three-day hike over a 5,500-foot pass.

After shopping for supplies and visiting missionary friends, Al and Nessie caught a train north. The eight-hour ride took them across the Central Luzon plain, through a sea of rice fields and peasant villages, and ended in the coastal town of San Fernando by the South China Sea. There they hired a driver to take them farther north along the coast to Tagudin where they spent the night. The next morning the driver took them inland to the Abra River. Expert rafts-men poled them safely across the swift-flowing river to Laganilang, where eight *cargadores* met them for the trek to Balbalasang. The *cargadores* had brought along a few packhorses, plus one for Al and Nessie to take turns riding.

Although it was not yet noon, the sky at Laganilang began to darken, and Al became anxious. Was this the beginning of a late-season typhoon, he wondered? The rainy season in northern Luzon began in June and usually ended in late October. Typhoons could strike at any time during those months, bringing torrential rains and strong winds. In Al's experience, the worst were those that appeared with little or no warning. There had been no inkling of an impending typhoon when he and Nessie left Manila.

After loading the packhorses and dividing the remaining supplies among themselves to carry, the *cargadores* were ready to start. The trail first took them along the Abra River before cutting away and up into a series of grass-covered hills, each higher than the one before. As Al had expected, it began to rain. He and Nessie donned their rain gear. The *cargadores* wore raincoats of woven palm fronds draped over their shoulders and water-resistant hats made from large gourds. The rains brought out leeches, which attacked horses and humans alike. The leeches found Nessie's raincoat to be a formidable barrier, but a few crawled as high as her neck, and Al pulled them off for her. Wearing shorts, Al was more vulnerable. He bled for hours from the leech bites.

Because of the rain, Nessie saw little of the region's beauty—grass-covered hills bracketed by groves of bamboo, then, as they climbed higher, range after range of mountains. Once they entered the rainforest—where even fern trees grew to thirty feet—the immense trees protected them from the intensifying wind. Nessie focused her attention on the muddy trail, but she still managed to slip frequently. Al encouraged her to ride the horse, which wasn't much larger than a pony. She did, and to her and Al's amusement, her feet dangled just off the ground.

As they climbed higher, they found themselves in a pine forest. The tops of the trees swayed in the wind, and the trail, which skirted the edge of the mountains, was carpeted with pine needles. Night would fall before they reached the village of Segub where they would have a roof over their heads. To light their way, *cargadores* chopped pine pitch kindling from saplings. The trail was so narrow that a slip in the dark would have meant a slip into eternity.

A vociferous barking welcomed them to Segub. All the inhabitants rose to greet the *Padji* and his new wife, "Mrs. *Padji*," who was neither feeling nor looking her best. Al greeted them warmly in Tingguian, then turned his attention to Nessie, helping her remove her wet and muddy boots. The pitched roof of the hut they were led to for the night reached the ground and kept out the rain and wind. The floor of the hut was dry, packed earth. After a quick meal of soup and Spam sandwiches (the *cargadores* dined on rice and sardines that Nessie had brought for them), Al and Nessie made a bed of Army blankets on the floor and were soon dead to the world.

When they reached Balbalasang two days later, Al learned from his radio that they had indeed trudged to Balbalasang in a typhoon. Torrential rains had washed out many mountain roads, delaying the several hundred dollars worth of supplies he had ordered on his way to Shanghai. The supplies had not yet arrived in Lubuagan, the capital of Kalinga, 56 kilometers to the east. Much to his chagrin, his cupboard was close to bare. For a week, Nessie prepared thin oatmeal for breakfast, Campbell's soup with a dash of rice for lunch, and rice garnished with soup for dinner—plus a small piece of wedding cake. They had brought a layer all the way from Shanghai.

On Sunday morning, the church bell rang at seven for the service that would begin at 7:30. Al neglected to tell Nessie that the bell would ring continuously for half an hour, so she left their house on the hill shortly after he did and descended to the church plaza. She entered the small church, painted light green and surrounded on two sides by bright red poinsettia, knelt to say her prayers, then sat on a low, backless bench, waiting for the congregation to arrive.

First came the small children, then the schoolchildren and young people, followed by mothers with babies slung in blankets on their backs, and finally the men and old people. Women sat on one side of the aisle, and men on the other. The church filled to overflowing. The last to arrive squatted in the aisle and on the steps that led down into the plaza. Babies left little puddles on the floor. Dogs wandered in and out, occasionally fighting.

Al conducted the service in Tingguian. He wore a richly embroidered chasuble while the acolytes wore red vestments. A collection of bright zinnias graced the altar. Unaccompanied, the congregation sang the "Missa de Angelis." As they worshipped, incense gently wafted through the sanctuary windows.

After the service, Al introduced Nessie to Chief Puyao and the members of his congregation. With shy smiles, each shook her hand, one or two placing an egg in her palm and whispering as they did so, "My Christmas to you, Mrs. *Padji*."

**Al and Nessie Griffiths in their Balbalasang home
shortly after their marriage.**

Al and Nessie soon found that their life took on a pleasant pattern. Each morning, Nessie would attend Al's early morning mass. While Al visited parishioners and attended to his church work, Nessie supervised the household, planned meals, and wrote letters to her family. Early each afternoon they took a short siesta. Then Al and the schoolteachers met on the school plaza for a tennis match. At five Nessie and Al had tea. When villagers returned from working in their fields, the church bell rang for vespers. Each evening after the service, Al and Nessie walked through Balbalasang to visit villagers and watch them engage in a variety of activities. Women pounded rice and wove baskets. Boys and girls tended livestock. Blacksmiths shaped head axes, spears, and machetes. At eight, they returned home for dinner.

As weeks went by, Nessie noticed that villagers always asked Al the same question. Finally, one evening she asked him what it was.

He told her what she was beginning to suspect—they were inquiring if she were pregnant.

"And what do you tell them?"

"Oh, not for twelve years!"

For the first six months of her pregnancy, Nessie was under the expert care of the mission nurse, Dottie Taverner. She reminded Nessie of her own mother who was from Scotland. Usually in good spirits, Dottie could be stern on occasion. She managed the dispensary with her able assistant, Anne Duñgo, a Balbalasang villager who had trained at the Episcopal Church's St. Luke's Hospital in Manila. The two treated an average of twelve thousand patients a year, many from distant villages.

In the seventh month, Dottie advised Nessie to go to Manila so she could give birth at St. Luke's Hospital. She cautioned Nessie not to do much walking on the trek out. Consequently, it took days to prepare for the trip. A village carpenter fitted a rattan armchair with a comfortable footrest and an awning for shade and protection from the rain. He fastened the chair securely to two long, thick bamboo poles. The eight men who would take her out came up to the house to practice. Four would carry her at a time; then the other four would take over. On the actual trip, they became so expert at this that they could perform the shift without putting her down. Through streams, along rainforest paths, and in and out of bamboo groves and pine forests they went. Ironically, the most difficult part of the trip for Nessie was the nine-mile Jeep ride from the Abra River to Bangued, and the subsequent bus ride to Manila.

Katharine was born December 11, 1939. Five weeks later, Al and Nessie, accompanied by Anne Duñgo, made the return trip to Balbalasang. Many villagers came to greet them while they were still far away. They escorted them to the riverside where more villagers awaited them, then up to the door of their house where Nessie removed Katy from the bamboo basket slung on a bamboo pole and covered with mosquito netting. From that moment on, Katy was on display whenever she was in the living room. Village women enjoyed watching Nessie give Katy a baby bottle or feed her orange juice from a spoon.

It wasn't long before Katy began to toddle about. A villager gave Katy a chicken, and she adopted it as a pet. When it wasn't following her, Katy insisted on carrying it like a baby in a tiny blanket slung from her shoulder. She and her *manok* were inseparable.

One day as Katy was having her bath, Nessie found

Hilda and Maymaya examining her belly button. Hilda was Katy's *amah* (nanny), and Maymaya was the houseboy.

"What in the world is the matter?" Nessie exclaimed.

"She is always touching it," said Maymaya, "so we thought she might have lice from the *manok* in it!"

Katy with two village friends, circa 1941.

IMPENDING WAR

IN JULY 1941, the U.S. Navy mined Manila Bay. All ships had to be escorted in and out. In August, radio reports were so pessimistic that Al thought war might start at any moment. Yet Bishop Binsted and his wife, accompanied by the U.S. High Commissioner to the Philippines Francis B. Sayre, were planning a visit to Balbalasang in October. Perhaps, Al thought, the political situation was not as bad as the radio reports indicated.

In September, a mining engineer by the name of Walter Cushing stopped in Balbalasang en route to his mine at Baay in Abra. He told Al he had heard about him and expected to see a bearded priest, not a young man with a family. Al and Nessie put him up in the dispensary that served as the mission's guesthouse. Cushing stayed for two days, the first Westerner Al, Nessie, and Dottie had seen for several months. They enjoyed his company, especially when he showed them how to pan for gold in the Saltan River. Unfortunately, his efforts were not successful.

At thirty-four years old, Cushing[4] was a dashing figure with striking good looks. His father was Canadian and his

---

[4] Ordun, M.B., *Walter M. Cushing: Guerrilla Leader and Hero of the Ilocos Provinces,* pp. 1-2.

mother Mexican. Slight in stature, he had dark skin and bright blue eyes. His parents met while his father was employed at a silver mine in Mexico. The family moved to Los Angeles, where Walter, the oldest of 10 children, graduated from high school. In the 1930s, two of Walter's brothers went to the Philippines to work in the gold mines. Walter wanted to join them, but he was married, the father of a child, and broke. He got a job as a steward on the *President Hoover* and jumped ship when it reached Manila. Once he found work, he sent for his family.

The subsequent failure of his marriage spun Walter into a nine-month drinking binge. To sober up, he planned to set sail for Saigon and join the French Foreign Legion but his friend, "Pee Wee" Ordun, intervened. Pee Wee persuaded Walter to join him in opening the Rainbow Mine in Baay, Abra.

In October, Al and Nessie found themselves in a three-ring circus preparing for Bishop Binsted's visit. While Al hired *cargadores* and organized supplies for their guests' trek to Balbalasang, Nessie cleaned house and helped Dottie make curtains for the dispensary. Dottie was afraid she was coming down with the flu. She didn't, but Al did. With Al in bed, it was up to Nessie to get saddles and accouterments in order, three Army cots mended, and innumerable other items ready for the *cargadores* to take out to meet the incoming guests.

On top of these minor trials, Chief Puyao's son-in-law was dying of cancer. For two months, he had been at St.

Luke's Hospital in Manila. When nothing more could be done for him, he was brought home, and the Chief called forth his relatives to attend a feast in his honor. A *carabao* (water buffalo) was slaughtered to feed guests. Hilda took Katy down to the village to watch the butchering. It was anything but a pretty sight—complete with dogs lapping up the blood. For the next several nights, Nessie had trouble getting Katy to fall asleep.

Despite the fact that Al still had a fever, he hiked to Talalong, a small village on the trail to Lubuagan, to greet the Bishop and his wife. Francis Sayre had come only as far as Bontoc, the capital of the Mountain Province, before returning to Manila. The political situation, the Bishop told Al, was too tense for Sayre to remain away from the Embassy.

Villagers turned out on the banks of the Saltan River to greet the Bishop and his wife as they entered Balbalasang. The highlight of his two-day visit was a confirmation service, followed by a feast, bonfire, and dance on the church plaza. To the spirited beat of brass *gansas* (gongs), the women, dressed in white skirts hemmed in red, and their hair adorned with strands of agate and carnelian, danced in line, waving their arms like birds in flight. The men, wearing red and black G-strings, brandished freshly sharpened spears, their thigh muscles rippling in tension as they pursued the women around the roaring bonfire. Even the Bishop and his wife took a twirl around the fire, much to everyone's delight.

The next morning, the Bishop and Al left for Balatok, Al's newest mission station. (The Bishop's wife remained behind to make the trip out via Talalong.) Al had cut a trail to Balatok up the steep mountainside behind the mission. He had sent young men ahead to clear the path and build a pine-branch lean-to for them to sleep under. Rain was coming down in sheets when they left, and that night on the mountain, they were soaked to the skin in spite of the lean-to. Leeches feasted on them. The next morning, the descent to Balatok was so precipitous and slippery that the Bishop had to lean on one of the *cargadores* the entire trek down, a matter of six hours. Nevertheless, he told Al he enjoyed every minute of the hike despite the hardships.

A few weeks later, Al received a letter from Bishop Binsted. "I know now," he wrote, "why everyone speaks with admiration and affection for Balbalasang... I was particularly impressed with the way Christianity seems to have worked itself into the lives of the people." In the same mail was a package from the Bishop's wife for Katy. It contained a large celluloid doll, one that moved its head, legs, and arms. The first Sunday, Katy insisted on taking it to church, where she removed both legs and arms, laid the doll on the bench in front of her, and announced in a large and clear voice, "*Natoy!*" which in Tingguian means "dead." Neither Nessie nor the villagers could suppress their amusement.

INVASION

ON SUNDAY, NOVEMBER 12, 1941, Al and Nessie celebrated their third wedding anniversary. In the morning, Nessie took Katy, almost two years old, to early mass. After the service, Al went to the dispensary to substitute for Dottie, who was on vacation in Manila, and Nessie returned home to cook—hard sauce for the plum pudding they were to have for dessert that evening, and raisin-drop cookies for Katy.

Every night they listened to the radio for news, and that evening they learned the U.S. Marines in Shanghai were prepared to leave on the *President* lines then in harbor. If they did, it was expected that all American civilians would also be ordered out, many of them to the Philippines. With the political situation becoming increasingly unstable, Al told Nessie to mail an emergency order for canned goods and supplies along with her usually large Christmas order. Nessie mailed a request for:

8 cases of milk (she had 5 on hand)
2 cases of soup
1 case of assorted stewed fruits for Katy
1 case of assorted vegetables for Katy
1 case of applesauce
1 case of quick Quaker oats
1 large carton of matches

In case they had to evacuate quickly, Al and Nessie packed a *pasiking* (Tingguian backpack) with a change of clothing, a raincoat, and an extra pair of shoes each, a five-pound tin of powdered milk, two tins of oatmeal, matches, and a flashlight. The opportunity came much sooner than they expected.

Within 24 hours of the attack on Pearl Harbor, the Japanese landed an advance force of 2,000 men at Vigan, a coastal town eighty kilometers directly west of Balbalasang.[5] Lowlanders fled into the mountains. Schools closed and children made their way home as fast as they could. An officer commanding a company of Filipino soldiers in the neighboring province of Abra found his way to Balbalasang and reported to Chief Puyao that his soldiers had deserted. Rumors spread rapidly: all the Chinese merchants in Vigan had been hanged, and the Roman Catholic nuns in Bangued raped.

On the fourth day of the war, Al and Nessie heard a knock on their door while they were eating dinner. Opening the door, Al was surprised to see two American aviators, Lieutenants Hausman and Sheppard, who greeted him by saying, "We suppose you have heard we bailed out of our planes in Bangued?"

"No," Al replied. He had heard practically everything else but not that. He invited them in to have dinner and spend the night.

---

[5] Norling, Bernard, *The Intrepid Guerrillas of North Luzon*, p. 23.

Dottie Taverner at her Balbalasang home.

The next morning, they left for the Batong-Buhay mine via the same trail Al and Bishop Binsted had taken to Balatok—straight up the mountain behind the mission. At the mine was a shortwave radio they hoped to use to contact their commanding officers.

Al provided each of the men with a horse to ride up the steep mountain. He cautioned the *cargadores* accompanying the officers to watch them closely. They knew how to pilot a plane, he said, but not much about riding horses.

Lieutenant Sheppard ascended no more than a hundred meters when his horse slipped. A *cargador* grabbed him and just managed to free his feet from the stirrups before the horse catapulted down the mountain at terrific speed, crashing into Al's chicken pen, and breaking its back. The Lieutenant came running down the mountain, concerned about the horse.

He remarked that this experience had been more frightening than bailing out of his plane over Bangued. Both men decided to hike rather than ride, and once more bade Al and Nessie goodbye. Al had the horse killed.

Al and Nessie listened to the radio at every opportunity. Not yet sensing the seriousness of the situation, they believed that help was on the way. As the days went by and American forces made such a gallant stand against the enemy on Bataan, they kept their hopes high and prayed that help would soon arrive. But, on December 22, 43,000 more Japanese soldiers, under the direction of General Homma, landed at Lingayen Gulf and quickly moved south to oppose American forces defending Bataan and Corregidor. [6]

---

[6] *Ibid*, p. 23.

SAFE IN A PHILIPPINE SHANGRI-LA

ONE EVENING BEFORE CHRISTMAS, just as Al and Nessie and their dinner guest—Dottie—were sitting down to eat, a villager burst into the house with the news that an American family was approaching Balbalasang—and that the mother was about to give birth. Dottie jumped up, grabbed a kettle, and placed it on Nessie's wood-fed stove to heat. Within minutes, Garnett and Dolly Morris and their five-year-old daughter, Denis, arrived. Much to Dottie's relief, Dolly was not in labor.

Garnett operated a small gold mine 40 kilometers west of Balbalasang. As the Japanese moved inland from the coast, he was afraid to keep his family there any longer. A tall man, Garnett towered over his diminutive—and very pregnant—wife.

Al suggested that the Morrises rest for a few days before continuing on to Batong-Buhay, where they could be with fellow miners and, more importantly, the services of a physician were available. Instead, they chose to stay in Balbalasang and, at Dottie's invitation, settled in on the upper floor of her home.

Al and Nessie's next visitor was Walter Cushing. Not having forgotten the fun they had panning for gold on his last visit, they were delighted to see him again. His gold mine in Abra was very near Garnett's. Walter said he had just gone to the coast to observe the movements of the Japanese. He was now on his way to Batong-Buhay to radio the U.S. Army Headquarters on Bataan for approval to organize a guerrilla company. He had gathered weapons and ammunition deserting Filipino Army units had left behind, and had hidden them in a tunnel at his mine.

Al showed Walter the trail he had cut to Batong-Buhay. No sooner had Walter headed up the mountain than his mining partner, Pee Wee Ordun, arrived. Pee Wee confided to Al that he was not in favor of Cushing's plan to organize a guerrilla company. He was particularly annoyed that Cushing had burned most of the mining equipment and the bamboo houses they had constructed for their laborers. Cushing's rationale was that he didn't want the Japanese to use them. Pee Wee was sure the smoke would attract the Japanese—and that they were probably already on their way to the mine to investigate. He was concerned they might find the hidden arsenal.

On Christmas Eve, Cushing returned to Balbalasang from Batong-Buhay. With great excitement, he reported that he had received permission to organize a guerrilla company, the first formed in northern Luzon to fight the Japanese. From the mine, he brought boxes of chocolates for Nessie, Dottie, and Dolly, all-day suckers for Katy and Denis, and several five-pound tins of powdered milk. The Morrises had arrived in Balbalasang with a live turkey, so they were all looking forward to a fine Christmas—in spite of the fact that the Japanese were now in control of the neighboring province of Abra to the west. Cushing was in a rush to return to his mine in Abra and did not stay to celebrate, although Pee Wee did, taking up residence in the guest quarters at the dispensary.

Christmas morning dawned cool, clear, and bright. Both the mission and the village were bright with red poinsettias. The first missionary to Balbalasang had planted them by the church. Villagers had taken cuttings to plant by their homes. Now the decorative plant seemed to grow everywhere, lending a festive glow to the Saltan River valley.

Al celebrated Christmas mass at eight. The church was full to overflowing. After the service, Dottie entertained younger village children with a party and gifts at her house while Al and Nessie entertained older children at theirs. Nessie decorated the living room with colorful balloons. On a table in the center of the room were gifts sent from churches in the United States. Each year Balbalasang children made miniature baskets, sugarcane mills, plows, fishing traps, mortars and pestles, and nose flutes to send to churches in the United States. In turn, the churches sent knives, dolls, scarves, jewelry, balls, and other American toys to the Balbalasang mission. The party ended with the distribution of gifts—plus candy Al had ordered—and a big peanut scramble down the terraced hillside to the church plaza below. With cries of "Merry Christmas," the youngsters returned home.

At eleven, Nessie put the Christmas turkey in the oven, and she and Al then sat down for a late breakfast. Al had just blessed their food when he and Nessie were startled to see from their living room window the women and children who had been at Dottie's house running across the church plaza screaming, *"Hapon! Hapon!"*

A villager rushed to the house to tell Al that a man from the neighboring village of Inalangan had arrived on horseback with the news that Japanese soldiers were only two kilometers away. Al grabbed the emergency *pasiking,* Nessie a blanket and an orange, and Hilda swooped up Katy.

Dottie, the Morrises, and Pee Wee ran to join them, and they all took off on the trail to Batong-Buhay. Al led them up the mountain, as he alone knew the trail. Garnett Morris and Pee Wee both had guns. They remained behind to see what would happen. Once on top of the mountain, Al returned to the house, meeting up with Garnett and Pee Wee on the way. They reported the men thought to be Japanese soldiers were in fact lowlanders. One was a man named Concepcion. Chief Puyao wanted Concepcion executed then and there for his failure to halt on the outskirts of the valley where the Chief had posted guards. Pee Wee intervened and convinced the Chief to change his mind.

Al returned to the mountain to bring the women and children home. Rushing into the kitchen, Nessie was relieved to see the turkey was in fine shape. She set to work baking a cherry pie for dessert.

When Al, Nessie, and their guests—Dottie, the Morrises, and Pee Wee—finally sat down for Christmas dinner, Al amused them by reading a Christmas note from an old friend in Massachusetts. His friend wrote that he would have to bear the brunt of war if it should come— while Al could live peacefully among his Tingguian friends and watch the clouds roll by day-by-day—safe in his Philippine Shangri-La.

Little did any of them know while feasting that day that all of them would be imprisoned during the war, three would perish, and it would be years before those who survived would be rescued. Walter Cushing himself would be shot and killed in an ambush in less than a year.

FROM *PADJI* TO LIEUTENANT

AFTER RETURNING TO HIS MINE IN ABRA, Walter Cushing sent Al messages to be delivered to various Army officers in the Mountain Province, and some to be transmitted to U.S. Army Headquarters on Bataan by the radio at Batong-Buhay.

Within days, Cushing returned to Balbalasang to ask Al to organize a guerrilla company. He wanted Al to prevent Japanese troop movements from Abra in the west to the town of Balbalan in the east. Guerrillas would also carry dynamite from Batong-Buhay to the lowlands where Cushing would use it to blow up bridges and roads to slow General Homma's advance on Manila. He needed all the dynamite he could get from the Batong-Buhay mine.

While on home leave in the summer of 1940, Al had been commissioned as a chaplain in the U.S. Army Reserve. Although he was a noncombatant, he agreed to help organize the 121st guerrilla company. He worried that Bishop Binsted would not approve, but there was no way to seek his advice now. All Al could do was pray he would do his best for his God and country.

Cushing gave Al the rank of Lieutenant, and asked Chief Puyao and the villagers to address Al as "Lieutenant" rather than their familiar "*Padji*." Al was to take his orders from Colonel John Horan. The Commandant of Camp John Hay in Baguio, Horan had been caught away from his company when the war broke out, and had fled to Lubuagan. There he lived with the Rev. and Mrs. Nagel at the Kalinga Academy.

Al asked Chief Puyao's son-in-law, Santos, to be his first lieutenant, and Frederick Dao-ayan, a villager who taught at the elementary school, to be his second lieutenant. Al used the school building as the headquarters for the 121st. Within days, thirty-seven Balbalasang men joined the company.

While he organized his guerrilla unit, Al continued with his church work, and had an evacuation camp built beside the Mapga River, about a mile from Balbalasang. Hidden in a sheltering pine grove, the cabin included three bunk beds, a table and benches, and a kitchen. There was a smaller house for Hilda, as well as an outhouse. Nessie, Katy, and Hilda camped at Mapga while the cabin was being built. They swam and fished in the river and cooked over an open fire. Nessie enjoyed herself immensely, despite the upheaval in their lives.

At dawn on January 19, Cushing and his men attacked two convoys of Japanese soldiers when they entered the coastal town of Candon in the province of Ilocos Sur. Sixty-nine Japanese were killed and fourteen trucks were captured or destroyed. The raid was "the heaviest blow the Japanese suffered anywhere in North Luzon in the first month of World War II."[7] News of Cushing's success soon reached Colonel Horan, who promptly proclaimed him a major in the guerrilla resistance.[8]

Cushing seized large supplies of food at Candon, including fifty bags of flour. Al's guerrillas carried the flour to Balbalasang, where he dispensed it to civilians and guerrillas as needed. He had forty bags transferred to Mapga. Much of the flour, Nessie discovered, was infested with weevils. Whenever any was needed, she and Hilda would spend a morning sifting it. They gave extra special care to the flour Al sent to Father Albert, the Roman Catholic priest in Salegseg, who used it to make communion wafers.

Little Denis Morris came out to Mapga with her *amah* to stay overnight when Dolly went into labor. A much-relieved and very proud Garnett hiked out the next afternoon with the news that Dolly had given birth to a big boy, Garnett, Jr., and both mother and son were fine. Dottie and Garnett assisted at the birth, the doctor from Batong-Buhay arriving an hour after it was all over. Only after the delivery did Garnett and Dolly share the news that the baby was to have been delivered by Cesarean section.

Colonel Horan arrived in Balbalasang for a visit with Al and the members of his 121st guerrilla company. Nessie hiked in from Mapga to prepare Al and the Colonel a

---

[7] Norling, Bernard, *The Intrepid Guerrillas of North Luzon*, p. 2.
[8] Ibid, p. 3.

noonday dinner. She opened their last tin of ham and covered it with cranberry sauce before baking it. Then she opened two tins of cherries to make a pie. The Colonel was most impressed, remarking, "Now this is what I call real cherry pie. It's not gluey with cornstarch. It *runs!*"

Ambush at Lamonan

FEBRUARY AND MARCH WERE QUIET, but late in the afternoon one Sunday in April, Al received a message to report to Colonel Horan in Lubuagan at once. Al waited to leave until early the next morning. Instead of taking the main trail that led through Salegseg and Balbalan, Al and his two guerrillas took a strenuous shortcut over the mountains that enabled them to reach Lubuagan in one day rather than the usual two.

Al discovered that the Colonel had no urgent need to see him. He told Al he was having trouble getting his commission. U.S. Army Headquarters had no record of Al's appointment as a chaplain in the Reserves. Al had his appointment papers with him so Horan radioed his serial number to Headquarters.

Despite the lack of urgency, Al enjoyed being in the company of his compatriots. With the Nagels and Horan at the Kalinga Academy were James Greer and his wife, who were in charge of the Mt. Data Rest House, halfway between Baguio and Bontoc, an Army sergeant who had led an attack on the Japanese-held airfield at Tuguegerao, and two young privates who had escaped capture by taking to the mountains.

Meanwhile, back at Balbalasang, a runner came to Nessie with a message for Al from Major Cushing that the

Japanese—eight hundred strong—were on their way from Abra to Lubuagan.

Cushing planned to ambush the enemy at Lamonan, in the pine forest about twelve kilometers west of Balbalasang. Al was to evacuate all villagers at once. Since Santos was on a scouting mission for Al, Nessie sent for Frederick Dao-ayan and Garnett Morris. They decided to dispatch one runner to Batong-Buhay to radio a message to Colonel Horan and Al, and a second runner to take the shortcut to Lubuagan in case the radio at Batong-Buhay was not working. Dao-ayan also sent runners to villages along the trail, urging all villagers to evacuate and to take their food supplies and animals with them.

Nessie's anxiety grew by the minute. She kept herself busy packing—clothes, food, blankets, and Al's important papers. She filled five-gallon kerosene tins with canned foods and sealed them with Para wax. Maymaya carried them to his rice fields where he buried them under his granary.

Al arrived at seven that evening, near exhaustion from having hiked as quickly as he could over the rough mountain trail. The radio message had reached him as he and Colonel Horan were having an early morning breakfast. He and his guerrillas had left for Balbalasang immediately.

After Al showered and rested, Nessie served him a chicken dinner by candlelight. This would be the last meal they would eat together in their little grass-roofed house where Nessie had arrived as a new bride.

They planned to spend the night in the house and evacuate the next morning with Dottie and the Morrises. The guerrillas slept in the kitchen in case Al needed them. But Nessie could not sleep. The longer she lay awake, the more convinced she became that the guards Dao-ayan had posted on the trail to Abra were asleep.

At midnight, she woke Al and begged him to take her and Katy to Mapga. Al woke the guerrillas while Nessie took Katy from her crib and wrapped her in a blanket. She handed Katy to one of the guerrillas who carried her slung in a blanket on his back.

Despite its short distance from Balbalasang, Mapga was difficult to reach. The trail followed the swiftly flowing Mapga River. The midnight evacuees had to cross and re-cross it thirteen times. The air was still and balmy, the sky alight with stars. The rushing water and footsteps were the only sounds.

Just as they turned off the main path to go deeper into the forest, they saw the most brilliant shooting star streak across the sky, its golden tail seeming to hover for breathless seconds before disappearing beyond the rim of the mountains. Nessie hoped the shooting star was a good omen that all would go well for them.

At Mapga, Al and the guerrillas, using the light of pine torches, removed forty sacks of flour stored in the cabin to make room for Nessie and Katy, as well as for Dottie and the Morrises. Once the job was compete, Al and the guerrillas returned to Balbalasang where Al managed to get two hours of sleep before going down to the village to ask for volunteers to help evacuate Dottie and the Morrises. Garnett had already left for the ambush. Cushing had ordered Al to remain in Balbalasang until the village was completely evacuated, including all animals and *palay* (unhusked rice).

At Chief Puyao's direction, villagers had built themselves an evacuation camp high in the mountains at a place called Maatop. Fearing that the Japanese would steal their horses and eat their pigs, they were up before dawn, carrying food supplies and driving their animals up the paths to their hideaway.

By noon, Al had Dolly and her children on their way to Mapga, but Dottie insisted on remaining behind to pack her most cherished possessions. Meanwhile, Al helped Anne Duñgo pack medical supplies, which two of his guerrillas carried to Mapga.

Late in the afternoon, Dottie finally told Al she was ready to leave. Only then could Al, accompanied by one of his guerrillas, make his way up the mountain trail to Lamonan.

As they climbed higher, the trail became shrouded in clouds and a cool, heavy mist. Shortly, they met two young men headed back to Balbalasang. One handed a note to Al. On opening it, he found the note was from Garnett to Dolly. It read: "Dear Dolly, the Japanese are getting nearer. Our ambush is ready. I shall do my best."

Al added a note to Nessie: "Dear Nessie, I am on my

way to the ambush. I'll do my best for my country. Love, Al."[9]

When Nessie and Dolly received the note at Mapga, neither of them said a word. Shortly after nightfall they went to bed—Dolly and Denis in the upper bunk, Nessie on the lower, Katy in her own little bunk, and Dottie on an Army cot. But their sleep was interrupted by two sets of runners from Lamonan—the first bringing the knapsacks of American soldiers taking part in the ambush, and the second all the induction papers of the men of the 121st, every one of which had Al's signature as first lieutenant and inducting officer on it. Nessie wrapped both the knapsacks and the papers well to keep them dry and asked the runners to crawl under the cabin and bury them.

By the time Al and his companion reached the summit, the trail was very dark and they could hear gunfire in the distance. They pressed on, the gunfire getting louder and louder with each step. Suddenly, they heard voices and the sound of men rushing down the trail toward them. They stepped off the trail, not sure what to expect. Al was relieved to discover the voices belonged to Cushing, Garnett, and American soldiers and guerrillas who had participated in the ambush. An elated Cushing told Al the ambush had gone well.

Meeting no resistance on their long trek into the mountains, the Japanese made three fatal mistakes. First,

---

[9] Griffiths, Alfred L., *For God and Country*, p. 25.

they neglected to send scouts ahead. Second, the advance guard marched close together, perhaps unnerved by the sights and sounds of a Southeast Asian rainforest. Third, the soldiers placed their helmets over the ends of their guns to protect the weapons from the mist.

When the lead soldiers were only a few feet away, Cushing opened fire and simultaneously set off dynamite charges. The Japanese were slaughtered. Those who made it through the initial assault were disoriented and ended up firing at each other, while Cushing and his men fled. The next morning, survivors hastily buried the dead in shallow graves and retreated with their wounded to Bangued, the provincial capital of Abra. None of Cushing's guerrillas was injured or killed.

How many Japanese died at Lamonan is not clear from the few existing accounts of the ambush. Pee Wee Ordun, who was later captured by the Japanese and imprisoned at Cabanatuan, wrote a nine-page description of Cushing and his guerrilla activities. According to Ordun, seven thousand Japanese marched into Abra after the fall of Bataan in April 1942. About a thousand hiked from Bangued to Lubuagan, their trail taking them right through Balbalasang. "On their way, Cushing met them in two or three ambuscades," Ordun writes.[10] In one of these ambushes, the Japanese fired on their own men. No doubt, this was the ambush at Lamonan.

---

[10] Ordun, M.B., Walter M. Cushing, *Guerrilla Leader and Hero of the Ilocos Provinces*, p. 5.

The American historian, Bernard Norling provides a more detailed account of the Lamonan ambush in his book, *The Intrepid Guerrillas of North Luzon:*

> One of Cushing's most spectacular coups took place on April 17, 1942, when he ambushed a company of the Japanese 122nd Infantry near Balbalasang in Kalinga Province... The enemy, overconfident and unheeding as they often were early in the war, marched into a defile in a column of fours. The ambushers opened fire, inflicting substantial casualties on the leading elements. Meanwhile, a Japanese company in the rear tried to outflank the guerrillas but became confused in the dark and opened fire on its own advance guard instead... The intramural battle among the Japanese continued until an estimated 160 of the enemy were killed.[11]

Al, Cushing, and the guerrillas reached Balbalasang at ten in the evening. Al took them up to his house and cooked them a meal with food Nessie had left behind. He sent a runner to Lubuagan with a message for Colonel Horan that the ambush had been a success. Both he and Cushing expected the Japanese to continue their push to Lubuagan. When the Japanese would arrive in Balbalasang on their way—and what they might do to retaliate for the ambush—was anybody's guess.

Before leaving for Mapga with Cushing, Garnett, and the other Americans who had taken part in the ambush, Al

---

[11] Norling, Bernard, *The Intrepid Guerrillas of North Luzon*, p. 8.

took a quick look around his house. It was still full of his and Nessie's possessions, including her *American Cookbook*. One of the guerrillas, Sergeant Goldbrum, thought the book was definitely an item that should be saved, so he went outside in the darkness and hid it in the grass. Two of Al's guerrillas offered to hide Nessie's teakwood chest, which was filled with linens and other treasures. Al told them that they could have anything else still left in the house.

Al and his companions didn't reach Mapga until four in the morning. They awoke to a breakfast of fresh scones and hot oatmeal prepared by Nessie, Dottie, and Dolly. Cushing ate his quickly. He was anxious to leave for Batong-Buhay to dismantle the radio there before the Japanese could find it. With the exception of Sergeant Heuser and Sergeant Goldbrum, Cushing ordered the American soldiers who had participated in the ambush to join guerrilla units hiding in the mountains, concerned that they were too big a drain on Al's meager resources. Heuser and Goldbrum were to remain temporarily at Mapga, guarding the camp from a spot down the path halfway to Balbalasang.

A camp Al had built for five now housed ten, and it included quite a menagerie—Al and Nessie's cat, the Morrises' dog, two-dozen chickens, and two goats. The goats were Al's pride and joy—and such great pets. One was a pregnant nanny and the other a handsome black-and-white billy. The nanny was a bit shy of all the noise and the people, but the billy loved company. On rainy days, he would run for the cabin, leap on to Katy's bed, and resist all efforts to dislodge him. In dry weather, he liked to sleep in the toilet shelter. One evening, when Nessie was wending her way there in the gloom, she entered—only to back out in a hurry when a male voice said, "Just us goats, ma'am."

On the Sunday after the ambush, Al was surprised to have a number of young people from other evacuation camps come out to Mapga for a communion service. Later that afternoon, a villager arrived in camp with the news everyone had been expecting: the Japanese had reached Balbalasang. All those hiding at Mapga knew they were in great danger. To this point, the Balbalasang people had been very loyal to them, but now that the Japanese were in control of the village, they weren't sure what to expect.

No to Surrender

MONDAY EVENING, after a long, worrisome day about what the Japanese might be doing in Balbalasang, everyone went to bed early. Sergeants Goldbrum and Heuser were on guard at their station when they saw two bright lights coming down a steep mountainside near them.

Sergeant Goldbrum ran back to camp and woke the Mapga refugees. They decided to flee up a small mountain stream behind the camp. Nessie started off first with Katy, Hilda, and the Morrises' *amah*, Gloria, who carried little Gerry and Denis. Al followed a few minutes later with Dolly and Dottie and their emergency provisions. Garnett and Sergeants Goldbrum and Heuser remained behind to assess the situation.

Although it was not raining, the underbrush was wet and covered with leeches. Nessie, Hilda, Gloria and the children struggled up the mountain, following the tiny stream in the pitch-blackness as closely as they could. When they reached a dry spot high above Mapga, Nessie realized she could go no further. She was in the first months of a pregnancy that she had kept secret from everyone except Al, but she had begun to bleed and was afraid she would miscarry.

Al reached her hours later, reporting that he had found

a good hiding place for Dolly and Dottie further down the mountain. When Garnett didn't catch up with him, Al had hiked back to Mapga to find out what had happened. On the way, he ran into Garnett. He hadn't been able to follow Al's trail, but he had good news. The lights Goldbrum had seen were the torches of two village men from Batong-Buhay with a message for Al. Al wanted to guide the women and children back to camp, but Nessie refused, insisting on spending the night on the mountain with Hilda, Gloria, and the children rather than risk sliding down the mountain in darkness.

The women and children slept close together and were warm, but the warmth was nothing compared to the heat of the reception Nessie received the next morning when she walked into camp and an anxious mother and nurse let loose at her for keeping the baby on the mountain all night. Garnett, Jr., was perfectly all right, but Nessie walked into the bushes and, letting Mother Nature finish what she had started the evening before, miscarried.

The Japanese took three weeks to march through Balbalasang on their way to Lubuagan. There were approximately 800 of them, although they marched through in small groups. They had Filipinos and captured American soldiers carrying their supplies. These men, who had to carry heavy packs barefoot over stony trails, suffered untold hardships.

A few villagers had made their evacuation camp across the river from Mapga. They slept beneath huge overhanging rocks and a few temporary shelters. At night, they would carry pine torches to light their way through the forest and across the river until they came within a mile or two of their granaries built adjacent to their rice terraces. Then they would extinguish their torches, creep up to their granaries, and take as many bundles of *palay* as they could carry. In the early hours of the morning, the Mapga refugees could see them come by their cabin, their torches flaring. The women carried baskets of *palay* on their heads. The men had tied bundles of *palay* to bamboo poles that they carried across their shoulders.

The Mapga refugees' fear that the Japanese would find and capture them was relieved when they learned that the last Japanese soldier had left Balbalasang. Al and his lieutenant Santos quickly returned to Balbalasang to see how much damage the Japanese had inflicted on the mission and the village. In Al's house, and also Dottie's, soldiers had smashed windows, torn pictures from the walls, stuffed newspapers down the toilets, and defecated in all the rooms. At the church, they had ripped the Stations of the Cross from the walls, torn apart the sacristy where the vestments, hymnbooks, and vestments were stored, and used the altar as a butcher block for the chickens and pigs they stole from villagers. They littered every village house they occupied, and ordered villagers to cut down coconut and banana trees so they could more easily get the fruit.

Dispirited, Al returned to Mapga. Cushing arrived from Batong-Buhay with news that dispirited him even more: General MacArthur had fled to Australia, and Corregidor had fallen to the Japanese on May 6. General Jonathan Wainwright—who had surrendered on Bataan in April—had ordered all forces resisting the Japanese to surrender. Colonel Horan had already done so in Lubuagan—on June 2—and had sent a message to Al via Cushing that if he decided to surrender, he should hike to Lubuagan carrying a white flag.

That night the small band of refugees at Mapga sat around their campfire, all rather depressed. Singing a few of their old favorites didn't improve their spirits. None wanted to surrender. Each knew too much about the guerrilla movement to risk being interviewed by the Japanese. They decided that if the Japanese wanted them, they would simply have to come and get them.

In the morning, Cushing announced he had decided to establish his guerrilla headquarters at an abandoned mine near Guinguinabang—a two-day hike from Balbalasang. He ordered Al to cease his guerrilla efforts and have the 121st company hide its military equipment. In the present state of affairs, Cushing felt it was useless to antagonize the Japanese. Before he departed—after a mass Al celebrated in the church—he told villagers not to address Al any longer as "Lieutenant" but to use their familiar "*Padji*."

HIDING IN THE FOREST

BY JUNE 1942, the Japanese had rounded up most American civilians in the Philippines—miners, missionaries, teachers, students, and entrepreneurs—and placed them in prison camps—Santo Tomas, Los Baños, and Camp Holmes, among others. Altogether, the Japanese incarcerated approximately 5,000 American civilians[12]. Almost all had surrendered to the Japanese willingly. Only a handful tried to escape imprisonment.

The Japanese had a special reason for wanting to capture the *Padji* and his family, revealed in a report written by Concepcion, a lowlander who had been educated at Cornell University. Concepcion was a spy for the Japanese. His report reads:

> Father Griffiths has never been an active military man, but he has great moral influence over the people of Balbalasang, who are a warlike tribe obeying old Puyao blindly... If Griffiths, who is with his family, surrenders, it is most likely he will be able to persuade the Balbalasang people to return to their village (from their evacuation camps), and thus normalize the rest of Kalinga. Kalinga is liable to be yet a "trouble area" unless controlled in time. Civilian

---

[12] Cogan, Frances B., *Captured: The Japanese Internment of American Civilians in the Philippines 1941-45*, p. 12.

travelers find staying in Kalinga villages very dangerous unless one is accompanied by an American.[13]

When Al learned that the Japanese were sending his friend, Rev. Nagel of the Kalinga Academy, to Balbalasang to ask him to surrender, he decided to leave the comfortable camp at Mapga and hide elsewhere. He knew Nagel would have no trouble finding a villager to lead him to Mapga, and he did not want to see him. Chief Puyao advised Al to make his new camp at Masablang, west of Balbalasang, where villagers had rice terraces and large gardens. Al and his family, along with Dottie, could live in huts villagers used when working in their gardens and were welcome to help themselves to as much garden produce as they needed. Chief Puyao invited the Morrises to join him at his Maatop evacuation camp. Al did not want to involve them in his troubles.

Before leaving, Al, Nessie, and Dottie carefully examined their store of tin foods and decided what to take with them and what to leave for the Morrises. Then they rolled up their blankets and clothes and bade the Morrises good-bye.

Al's guerrillas helped with the move. Their route to Masablang first took them back to Balbalasang and then on to the small village of Inalangan. Masablang was in the

---

[13] Conception, "Report to Colonel Nakashima," p. 5.

forested mountains above Inalangan. Al's guerrillas built them two shelters in a bamboo grove about half a kilometer from the villagers' garden huts. One was for Al, Nessie, and Katy, and the other one was for Dottie. Neither could be seen by anyone working in the rice terraces or gardens.

For two months, their life was almost idyllic. Food was plentiful—a great variety of fresh vegetables and plenty of bananas, sugarcane, and coconut. The Saltan River flowed just two hundred feet from their camp, and they swam in its crystal clear waters every morning.

June brought the onset of the rainy season. The mornings were warm and sunlit. In the early afternoon, it would begin to cloud up and by three o'clock, there was a turbulent but brief thunder and lightning storm. By five o'clock, the sky had cleared. Everything was gleaming again, the air fresh and fragrant.

But the rainy season also brought typhoons, and the small band of refugees experienced two severe ones at Masablang with strong winds and heavy, heavy rains. Although their shelters shook from the wind, and the roofs leaked, they managed to stay dry. During the second typhoon, fifteen Japanese soldiers from the garrison at Lubuagan came to Balbalasang looking for Al. They arrived wearing G-strings, their uniforms folded in their raincoats. They stayed just one night before returning to Lubuagan the next morning. Villagers told Al that the officer in charge had questioned them about him. They told the officer that the *Padji* had been in Balbalasang but had left. The officer then went into the church to pray. As he and his soldiers were leaving, he said to the people, "Tell Father Griffiths to come back and teach Christianity."

It took a while for Al and Nessie to relax after this scare, but it wasn't long before they were again enjoying themselves in their isolated but lovely hideaway where they could see and hear the Saltan River rushing in its course through a forest of pine. Villagers occasionally brought them the meat of a wild pig or deer, which they ate with fresh corn and sweet potatoes baked in an open fire. Al built a shelter for the dozen or so chickens he had retrieved from Mapga, and once more, they had eggs for breakfast. Whenever Balbalasang villagers came to visit, they brought avocados from the mission trees. They were eating so well and beginning to feel so secure that Al dug a large plot to put in a garden.

And Al continued with his church work, although at a reduced pace, hiking in to Balbalasang to conduct Sunday services, baptizing infants, burying the dead, even visiting some outstations when his guerrillas assured him the trails were safe. And Dottie occasionally returned to her dispensary to care for villagers in need of medical attention. But venturing away from their hiding place at Masablang was risky, and in late August when Al's guerrillas reported two hundred Japanese were on their way to Balbalasang from Lubuagan, they ceased going anywhere. Surely, they were not coming for him, Al thought. He just wasn't that important. Perhaps they were on their way to Lamonan to give proper burial to the dead killed in the ambush months before. Nevertheless, when villagers sent news that the Japanese had arrived, Al was very anxious.

A CLOSE CALL

THAT NIGHT AL, NESSIE, AND DOTTIE played three-handed bridge in an effort to keep their minds off the Japanese. At last, they turned in for the night. At midnight, Katy cried, and Nessie got up to attend to her. She gasped when she looked out the window—coming up the trail was a long line of men with torches and they were heading directly to them. She woke Al. He crouched at the front of their shelter by the trail while Nessie and Dottie crouched at the back with Katy. They were very relieved when they saw the faces of village men.

"We have come to tell you that the Japanese are looking for you. They think you are nearby because the bed in the church is gone."

When the fifteen Japanese had arrived in Balbalasang during the typhoon, Dottie's bed had been stored in the church. Afterwards she sent for it. The Japanese noticed the bed was missing.

Al went to Dottie's shelter to wake her. Nessie begged the men to take them to a new hiding place, but they said there was no immediate danger as the Japanese had called for a meeting of all village officials at nine in the morning. They were sure the Japanese would do nothing until after the meeting. They promised to send men to evacuate them at dawn. The men returned to Balbalasang, and Al, Nessie, and Dottie went back to bed but could not sleep. During those sleepless hours, Nessie heard—as clearly as if she were in the room—her long-dead mother sing her favorite hymn, "Be Not Dismayed Whate'er Betide, God Will Take Care of You."

At three o'clock, they rose to prepare for their evacuation. Al carried a change of clothes for each, blankets, and food to the river's edge. The rest of their clothes and possessions they packed in suitcases to be temporarily hidden in the forest.

At four, two strong young men arrived to help. Al gave them the suitcases to hide. At five, Al and Nessie sat down for breakfast. The sun was just beginning to turn darkness into dawn when Martinez, one of the young men, dashed into camp shouting, "*Padji*, they are right behind me!"

Without uttering a word, Al grabbed Katy and ran to get Dottie. Nessie snatched up a blanket and two scones from the table as she flew out the door. Martinez carried the *pasiking*, which contained their clothes, food, and a large tin of powdered milk Nessie was safeguarding for Katy. They ran right through the river, clothes and all. As they climbed up the bank, Martinez stumbled, and the tin of powdered milk flew open, leaving a white trail for the Japanese to follow.

When they reached the point in the trail where Martinez and his companion had taken their suitcases, Al urged Nessie and Dottie to keep going while he helped the men hide the suitcases in a gully by covering them with ferns. Not wanting the men to suffer should they be caught with him, Al told them first to hide and then return to Balbalasang after the soldiers left.

As he rushed to catch up with the women, Al could hear the soldiers shouting and shooting, making a great noise in their pursuit. Inalangan villagers sent the Japanese up the wrong trail. Once the soldiers realized their mistake, it was too late. Al and the women had branched off the main trail to a small stream they followed a short way before cutting off into the forest and going straight up the mountain.

The way up was very precipitous, and they fell and slid often. They only stopped to rest when they could no longer hear the Japanese chasing them. The skies clouded over, and it began to rain. They were all soon drenched to the skin. In his rush to get away, Al had left behind in the gully their emergency *pasiking*. In it were their raincoats, some food, medicine, and cotton, and Nessie's small black bag that contained their insurance papers and the small amount of money they had.

Al gathered some large leaves and tried to make a shelter for them. Without his machete, his attempts were sketchy. Nessie gave Katy the two scones she had grabbed from the table. The rest went hungry. They sat huddled in the cold rain the rest of the morning.

In the middle of the afternoon, the sun came out and Al lit a fire so that they could dry themselves. Surprisingly, seemingly out of nowhere, an Inalangan villager appeared and asked Al if he would like him to cook them some squash. Al replied they would be very grateful to have some squash—that they were very hungry. The villager said he had a garden about a kilometer away. He apologized for not having any rice.

As they were eating the squash, three more men appeared, two of them complete strangers from distant villages. They told Al they had been sent by Santos to evacuate them. The Japanese had been so enraged by their escape, they said, that they burned not only their shelters at Masablang but also the shelters of the Inalangan villagers. When the Japanese returned to Balbalasang, they assembled the entire village, lighted a huge fire, and burned everything Al, Nessie, and Dottie had left at Masablang—including Dottie's bed.

With night drawing on, they partly retraced the trail they had taken. Al told the men where he had hidden their suitcases and the *pasiking*, and they went down the mountain to retrieve them. The men found the suitcases, but not the *pasiking*. The men then led Al and the women on a steep trail to the village of Uling, which is three kilometers from Balbalasang. They reached Uling at eight o'clock, after night had fallen. Villagers fed them and urged them to rest for a few hours before starting out again. Villagers begged them not to surrender to the Japanese. The Japanese had been so furious at their escape, they said, that they had sworn to kill them. Al assured them they would not surrender.

They rested until midnight. When they woke, it was raining again, but they could not delay their departure. Al had decided to establish a camp in Abra. That meant they had to take an overgrown trail that went up and over a 6,000-foot mountain. For one long stretch, they were in sight of Balbalasang, and could not use torches to light their way. Because of the rain, the leeches and mosquitoes were out in force. The darkness and the muddy trail caused them to slip often. Nevertheless, Katy slept soundly all the way up the mountain. One of the men carried her in a blanket on his back. She stirred only when he shifted her from one side to the other. When they reached the summit, Nessie fell by the side of the trail, exhausted and covered from head to toe with mud.

But it was dawn and the worst was over. Below them, from their vantage in Abra, they could see numerous villages—in many of them, Al had held services before the war. They reached the first village at eight in the morning. Villagers received them hospitably and prepared a welcome meal of rice, corn, eggs, and bananas.

They continued on to Duldulao, where the village chief received them hospitably and invited them into his home. While Al met with the chief, Nessie, Katy, and Dottie fell asleep on a large bed and didn't wake until early afternoon. The chief wanted them to stay in the village, but Al thought that unwise and instead accepted the chief's offer to hide in a mountain garden high above the village. The chief's men led them there after Al and the women cleaned up in a nearby stream and had lunch. There were a few huts at the garden. The men made the largest hut as comfortable as possible for the new occupants before returning to Duldulao at nightfall.

The next evening the small band of refugees was startled to hear voices approaching, but were relieved to see Balbalasang men—including the two youth who had helped them escape the Japanese at Masablang. The men brought distressing news: the Japanese, very angry at Al's escape, had returned to Balbalasang and burned all the mission buildings except the church. And they had taken thirty Balbalasang men as hostages, swearing to hold them in Lubuagan until Al surrendered.

That night the Balbalasang men slept in one of the garden huts. Al lay sleepless. He knew he had no choice but to surrender. After resting one more day, he returned with the men to Chief Puyao's camp at Maatop to inform the Chief of his decision.

DEEPER INTO THE FOREST

NESSIE WAS VERY ANXIOUS THAT DAY and the next, wondering if Al had reached Maatop safely. She and Dottie kept themselves busy washing clothes in a nearby stream. They wrapped themselves in blankets while their pants, shirts, and underclothes dried in the sun. Katy was oblivious to their plight. She enjoyed sunning on the rocks by the stream's edge and searching for minnows in the shallows. Nessie felt badly because she had shoes and Katy had none. Nessie had put her shoes in the missing *pasiking*.

Meanwhile, at Maatop, Chief Puyao's reaction to Al's decision was strong: he was adamant that Al not surrender. If he did, Puyao swore he would ambush the party on its way—for the Japanese had sworn to kill Al, and he would not let the Japanese carry out their threat. Furthermore, he said the *Padji* was not to worry about the hostages. He had sent word to them to escape, and he was sure they would succeed. He was correct. One night, not long after their capture, they eluded the Japanese-controlled Philippine Constabulary assigned to guard them, slipped away among the rice fields, and made their way back home to Balbalasang.

Living at Maatop with Chief Puyao and Balbalasang villagers was the Morris family. When Al described their plight, Dolly gave him a change of clothing for each of them. Nessie wept when she found that Dolly had also tucked in a pair of Denis's shoes for Katy.

Upon his return, Al realized they had to move. Too many people knew of their whereabouts. He made arrangements with two Balbalasang men he trusted, Manuel and Vicente, to guide them at night to a new camp deeper in the forest. Manuel carried Katy, Vicente their bedding, and Al packed the rest of their belongings. Fear gripped them when they had to pass through a village where Philippine Constabulary soldiers were posted. But Katy, who was awake, never made a sound, and the village dogs were mercifully silent.

Manuel and Vicente led them past the village to a tiny hut at the edge of rice fields. There they crawled in, spread their blankets on the reed floor, and curled up for a short rest. At dawn thy resumed their hike. For two hours, they climbed up and down mountains and in and out of pine forests until they came to a gully with a tiny stream. They walked up the stream until they came to a small clearing between two huge bamboo clumps. Manuel and Vicente cut bamboo, split it, made a floor, and erected roof supports for a lean-to. They only had time to add a temporary roof of banana leaves before returning to Balbalasang.

That night, the wind roared and the rain came down in torrents. Nessie hid Katy under Dottie's umbrella, while she, Dottie, and Al huddled under their blankets.

At dawn, Al crawled out of the hut and found some flat

stones, which he placed on the bamboo floor. He rigged green wood on them to hold their cooking pot, lit a small fire, and boiled some rice for their breakfast.

Manuel and Vicente returned later in the day for a few hours to roof the lean-to with cogon grass. This provided the band of refugees with better protection, but for five days, they had to weather the remnants of a tropical depression, rarely venturing from the lean-to.

Diwayan, as Manuel and Vicente called the camp, was their home for three months, from the end of September until Christmas. Twice a week, Manuel and Vicente brought them rice and such vegetables as they could—a little squash, a few beans, occasionally an egg for Katy, and a little salt. The salt was very precious. Balbalasang villagers purchased salt from lowland traders. Because of the war, traders were no longer making trips into the mountains. Salt was almost worth its weight in gold.

Once, when Manuel and Vicente were delayed, the refugees got quite hungry. Al ventured into the forest to forage and returned with the blossom of a wild banana, which Nessie boiled for them to eat.

Each day they bathed in the tiny stream. On warm days they would stretch stark naked in the sun, trying to absorb an extra bit of vitamin D. Occasionally, they would take short walks from camp. On one such jaunt, Al and Katy saw a band of monkeys, much to their delight.

Katy's pets were the polliwogs in a tiny stream pool. She spent hours trying to catch them in her hands. Once when she was sitting on her bed playing with Dottie's deck of miniature cards, a huge rat ran across her blanket. She gazed at it casually and went on playing.

With Dottie's cards, Katy learned to count and play a few simple games. Al, Nessie, and Dottie played countless rounds of rummy and three-handed bridge to while away the hours.

Their library consisted of Nessie's Bible and Dottie's small devotional books. They read them constantly. One memorable day, Manuel and Vicente brought books from the Morrises. One was a copy of Shakespeare. They read and re-read his plays. Another was a book on mining that they also read cover to cover.

This existence was more trying for Al than for Nessie and Dottie. He had been used to an exceedingly active life. Now he was confined to their small camp. He no longer had his church work, and the absence left hours on his hands when he had nothing to do. And it frustrated him that he knew nothing of what was going on in the guerrilla movement.

One night in early October, he set out with Manuel and Vicente for Cushing's camp on a mountain slope about eleven kilometers north of the village of Guinguinabang. Al found the going difficult. He had to stop several times to rest and regain his strength. His poor diet was taking its toll. On the way, he met a Roman Catholic priest whose news disturbed him greatly. The priest told Al that it was a shame he had left Balbalasang because the Japanese were allowing all missionaries to continue their work. Al wondered what Bishop Binsted's reaction would be when he learned that Al had chosen to do his duty to his country and join the guerrilla movement.

Al was disappointed to find that Cushing was not at Guinguinabang. Cushing was on a trip to the Cagayan Valley to contact a guerrilla unit. Nevertheless, Al enjoyed the company of Cushing's guerrillas, and he especially enjoyed listening to the shortwave radio for news from San Francisco. The confident tone of the broadcasters restored his hope that the war would soon be over. Each day the guerrillas mimeographed a news report ("The Echo of the Free North") and distributed it to towns and villages in Abra and Kalinga. Their goal was for the Filipino people to remain confident that the Philippines would be liberated and given full independence at the end of the war.

The guerrillas had planted a huge garden—but they were so sure help would arrive soon that they didn't expect to harvest it.

Concepcion, the lowlander Chief Puyao believed was a spy for the Japanese, was at the camp. He asked Al where he and his family were hiding, but Al declined to tell him.

What neither Al nor the guerrillas knew at the time— but were soon to find out—was that Cushing was dead. On September 19, in the town of Jones, Isabella Province, Cushing was ambushed by Philippine Constabulary troops collaborating with the Japanese. Severely wounded in the attack, Cushing shot himself with his Colt 45. His desire to take his own life rather than be captured so appealed to the Japanese code of honor that they gave him a funeral and buried him in the local churchyard.[14]

[14] Ordun, M.B., Walter M. Cushing, *Guerrilla Leader and Hero of the Ilocos Provinces*, p. 9.

CHRISTMAS AT MAATOP

AS THE SECOND CHRISTMAS OF THE WAR approached, Al and Nessie began to receive letters from the Balbalasang people urging them to visit their evacuation camp at Maatop so they could all celebrate Christmas together. Villagers were anxious to celebrate and make their communions.

Al and Nessie didn't need much persuading. They were weary of their three months' stay at Diwayan. The bamboo slats they slept on seemed to get harder all the time, and the hut had become infested with rats. The vermin made nests in the cogon grass roof, and at night Al and Nessie would wake to the squeals of their young.

In December, Chief Puyao invited Al, Nessie, and Dottie to spend Christmas at Maatop. They gratefully accepted his invitation, tired of their isolated life in the forest and eager to see the Chief, village friends, and the Morrises. After a full day of hiking, they reached Maatop late in the afternoon on December 23. Chief Puyao and his family greeted them warmly, and they wept as they embraced each other.

At Maatop, villagers had cut an immense clearing in the forest for their huts and gardens. Al was amazed to see that they had also built a huge two-story structure of bamboo and *runo* (a rigid grass), 30 feet wide and 100 feet long. The first floor would be used for Christmas services, Chief Puyao said, and the second as their guest quarters.

The Morrises' baby was thriving on a diet of soft rice and broth made from the meat guerrillas sent from their camp whenever they butchered. Garnett had cleared a large patch of ground for a garden. He was busy with that, and also learning how to weave from one of the men. Dolly occupied herself by making clothes for Denis and the baby. Denis had learned the Tingguian dialect and served as an interpreter for her parents.

Most villagers were still in Balbalasang harvesting rice, but they started to arrive at Maatop late in the afternoon on Christmas Eve and kept coming far into the evening. Carrying bundles of freshly harvested rice on their heads, they lit their way with pine torches when it grew dark. Many brought gifts for their guests—rice, coconuts, squash, and papayas. Food was so plentiful and the occasion so merry that Al, Nessie, Dottie, and the Morrises were almost convinced that peace had returned.

As the night air cooled—dipping into the high forties— villagers lit huge bonfires. Everyone gathered close around them and sang carols. Then the young people presented the Christmas drama in the Tingguian dialect. For the first time they staged and directed it themselves. Just a generation before, the villagers had never known how, "He had taken the form of a servant and was made in the likeness of man." Now they were celebrating the birth of the Christ child in their own unique and moving way.

Village women pounding rice to remove the husk from the grain.

Christmas morning Al celebrated Eucharist and he baptized all the children who had been born in the months of separation. When he asked one mother—one of the poorest in the village—what she had named her daughter, she replied, "We shall call her Joy, *Padji*."

Al, Nessie, and Dottie had often been hungry at Diwayan. But how they feasted that day! Their first course was rice with carabao meat and Chinese cabbage, their second was rice with sugar and coconut.

When she arrived at Maatop, Nessie was thrilled to find her teakwood chest. It had been hidden in the mountains since the beginning of the war, and villagers had carried it to Maatop. From it, Nessie took jade napkin holders her sister had sent her from China and hung them on a little Christmas tree as ornaments. Then she cut a white Tingguian *tapis* (wraparound skirt) in two and made a small one for Katy and another for Denis. She gave Katy a gold cross with pink flowers that Nessie's parents had given her on her confirmation.

In the afternoon, Chief Puyao called a meeting. Captains Perryam and Stevens, along with a few other guerrillas, had come over from their camp near Guinguinabang.

At the meeting, they spoke about how confident they were that the Japanese would be defeated. Recalling what he had heard on the radio when he visited the guerrilla camp, Al talked about how American submarines were operating close to the shores of Luzon, making it dangerous for Japanese craft to move in Philippine waters. He was confident that help would soon arrive.

Before Captain Perryam returned to his camp, he gave Al a twenty-dollar bill. He told Al he might need it someday for Katy.

Chief Puyao insisted that Al stay at Maatop rather than return to Diwayan. As an enticement, he gave him a large tract of land for a garden. Al was delighted. All day long, he chopped down small trees, cleared brush, and pulled up roots. Once the brush dried, he burned it. Villagers gave him sweet potato cuttings and a variety of seeds to plant. Al hoped to produce enough food to meet his and Nessie's needs, and he was thrilled when the first corn and bean seeds sprouted.

His and Nessie's moods couldn't have been better: they were safe, they were among friends, and they had good living quarters.

The rainy season had ended, the weather was glorious, and the mountain scenery—rim after rim of forested mountains stretching into the distance on all sides—took their breath away. But at the end of January, a guerrilla arrived at Maatop and asked for Al. His face was downcast. He handed Al a letter from Captain Hirano, the commanding officer of the Lubuagan garrison.

Al opened the letter quickly. It was two-pages, single-spaced, and typewritten. Hirano wrote that the Imperial Forces of the Japanese Army had captured all the islands in the Pacific. It was now impossible for MacArthur to return to the Philippines. He said he understood why Al had not surrendered, but if he did so now, he would transport him and his family to Camp Holmes near Baguio (where his American friends were "singing and chatting"), and arrange safe passage back to the United States.

He ended his letter with a warning: his patience had worn thin, and if Al didn't surrender immediately, he would be executed when captured.

The letter depressed Al. As he was translating it for Chief Puyao, another runner arrived with more bad news: Japanese troops had raided Guinguinabang and captured all the American guerrillas there. Furthermore, Japanese troops were on their way to Balbalasang from Abra. Al felt vulnerable. As long as the guerrillas could hide out, he had felt reasonably secure.

He told Chief Puyao that he would surrender. The Chief said that he would call a meeting with villagers to discuss the matter. "Let the people speak," he said. Later that day they did—and they insisted that their *Padji* not surrender. Al agreed to honor their request.

The *Padji* must go even deeper into the forest now, Chief Puyao said. And he must take two teen-age boys with him. He would be so far away from any village that there might be times when food would be scarce.

The boys knew how to fish for eels in the swift mountain streams and which plants and roots were edible. Al wasn't keen on the idea, fearing the Japanese would pressure the boys' families to reveal his whereabouts, but he also knew that he and his family and Dottie couldn't exist in the wilds alone, and he accepted the Chief's advice. John and Marcus, each about fifteen years of age, agreed to accompany them.

The "Good Luck" Camp

AL'S GUERRILLAS HELPED WITH THEIR EVACUATION. Once again, Nessie packed her teakwood chest and had it hidden in the forest. She, Al, and Dottie took with them just a few clothes, blankets, pots and pans, and machetes. And Katy. For a day and a half, they hiked through rugged mountain terrain and forded many fast-moving streams. They crossed into Abra where they decided to make their camp near a small brook about a hundred meters from a river.

In just a day, Al's guerrillas built them a large and comfortable house of bamboo and *runo*. As they were building it, they heard dogs barking, which meant that hunters must be nearby. A moment later, a deer ran right through their camp. The pursuing hunters speared it, and that night they all had venison for dinner. The hunters told Al his camp had brought them good luck. Al hoped it would do the same for him.

Whenever they heard dogs barking, they knew hunters were nearby. If the hunters were successful, they always gave Al and Nessie a haunch of venison or a bit of wild pig. They would turn the meat over a roaring fire until it was a succulent brown and dripping goodness.

The hunters butchered whatever they had speared on a large flat stone in the middle of the river, as a means of keeping their dogs at bay. One hunter would capture the blood in a vessel. Another would wash the meat in the swift-flowing stream. Everything but the hide and hooves the hunters carefully divided and packed away in their baskets or hung on sticks of wood to carry home. Hunters from Balbalasang always brought rice to Al and his family. They didn't mind the long journey because they said they always caught game at the *Padji's* "Good Luck" camp.

One day when Al heard dogs barking, he grabbed his spear and ran towards the sound. When he reached the river, he saw, much to his amazement, a large buck swimming downstream. He was so surprised by the sight that he forgot to throw his spear. When he regained his wits, the buck was gone. However, hunters speared it downriver. They were much amused at the *Padji's* attempt at hunting.

Wildlife abounded in the forest. During the night, Al and Nessie often heard a peculiar grunting sound, too coarse for the croak of a frog, unlike anything they had heard before. Marcus and John knew what the sound was— the grunts of a giant python.

The forest was also full of monkeys, and they often saw bands of them swinging through the trees. When he was out for a walk one day, Al surprised a band of brown and white monkeys at the river. The monkeys were almost as tall as his waist. Marcus and John treed a small brown monkey and tried to smoke it down so Katy could have it as a pet, but the monkey refused to budge. Katy did have a pet, however—a small brown hen that one of the hunters had given her. She named it Jenny and she liked carrying it in a blanket slung over her shoulder. Whenever Jenny laid an egg, Nessie would give the whole egg to Katy for dinner if the three adults had anything else to go with their rice. If not, Nessie carefully divided the egg into four so each of them could have a taste.

Since there were many wild chickens in the forest, Al borrowed a rooster and a chicken trap from one of the hunters and tried to catch some, using the roster as a lure. But there was something lacking in the "come hither" call of the rooster, and no curious chickens found their way into the trap.

Marcus and John often fished for eels in the river. The eels were as thick as a man's arm and more than a meter in length. Nessie and Dottie would boil them for dinner since they had no oil to fry them.

The small band of refugees found their life in the forest fascinating, and they would often accompany Marcus and John when they gathered edible plants, including the heart of a palm tree. Nessie and Dottie would slice and cook it like a vegetable. The palm was tasteless, but it filled their stomachs. Once they came across villagers looking for beehives and were the grateful recipients of a small tube of honey, a special treat.

Nessie and Dottie spent hours under a certain tree collecting hundreds of bright red seeds—and an equal amount of time searching for a means to soften them so they could string them as beads. They never discovered a method that worked. On other trees, they found solidified gum. Marcus and John said the gum was excellent for mending clay jars. Al discovered the gum burned slowly and well, and it gave off a sweet-smelling savor. Every evening, he would place a large chunk on a flat rock in their hut and light it. In the dark tropical night, they all felt comforted by its glow.

Gradually, they began to feel secure at their "Good Luck" camp. Nessie made herself a pair of pajamas out of a sheet, and then made a pair for Al. For the first time in months, they got out of their clothes when they went to bed. This was no small luxury. Every morning they had rolled up their blankets in case they had to make a quick getaway. Now they relaxed in their pajamas and left their beds made on the floor.

The refugees grew to like their life in the forest. As time passed, they became less afraid of being captured by the Japanese. Their food was not always varied or sufficient, but they were free, and they enjoyed good health. Every day they swam in the river. They could sit and shout as loudly as they wished, and they enjoyed the company of friends when they came to bring them food.

But on a Saturday morning in March, two boys, Juan and Bernadino, arrived in camp with the news that 200 Japanese troops, led by Captain Hirano himself, were on their way to Balbalasang from Lubuagan. Hirano had only one objective: to capture the *Padji*.

HERE THEY ARE!

BECAUSE A FEW HUNTERS KNEW the location of their camp, Al decided to move to a temporary camp two kilometers away. Juan and Bernadino returned to Balbalasang, promising to return when they had more news.

Four days passed. No news. On the fifth, Marcus and John noticed pieces of burned grass, bamboo, and *runo* drifting over the forest. They feared Captain Hirano had set fire to Balbalasang. Anxious, they told Al they wanted to return home, but he pleaded with them to stay, afraid they would be caught by the Japanese and forced to reveal his whereabouts. Al had defied the Japanese so many times that he was sure Captain Hirano would carry out his threat to kill him if captured. He could only pray that Nessie and Katy would be spared.

Ash stopped falling the next morning.

To keep their minds off what might be happening in Balbalasang, Al and Nessie helped Katy hunt for the nest Jenny made somewhere in the back of their lean-to. Searching carefully, Katy found it. She was jubilant: it contained four eggs, a treat indeed.

At that moment, Dottie shouted, "*Here they are!*"

Al grabbed Katy and joined Nessie and Dottie in front of the lean-to. Thirty Japanese troops faced them—guns and bayonets drawn. The lieutenant in command shouted at Al to raise his hands. Al quickly gave Katy to Nessie and obeyed the order. With the troops were the fathers of John and Marcus, ropes tied around their waists, forced at bayonet point to lead the troops to Al's hiding place.

Unable to contain their fear, John and Marcus bolted into the forest. The soldiers fired at them, and Al yelled at them to come back. The boys returned, trembling. The lieutenant slapped each of them harshly.

Soldiers snatched up Al's machetes and shouted at Nessie and Dottie to roll up their blankets and clothes. They bayoneted Nessie's pots and pans and set fire to the lean-to. They tied a long rope around Al's waist and then marched them all back to the main camp. There they tied Al to a machine gun and ordered him to remain standing. They shoved the women and Katy into the small hut that John and Marcus had used as their sleeping quarters.

Nessie barely had time to catch her breath when a soldier reached into the hut, grabbed Katy, and drew her outside. Very anxious, Nessie followed right behind. The soldier seated Katy on a large rock, put a rice bowl over her head, and cut her hair like that of a little Japanese girl, short and just below the ears. Katy made no outcry, much to Nessie's relief. (Although she was only three at the time, Katy remembers this incident, recalling that Nessie said to her: 'Don't cry. If you do, the soldiers will kill me.')

The Lieutenant ordered Nessie and Dottie to show him their books. Nessie handed him her Bible and Katy's Mother

Goose book. He glanced at the Bible without opening it and handed it back. The Mother Goose book amused him. He smiled at the illustrations and showed them to soldiers standing nearby before returning it to Nessie. Dottie then gave him her five devotional books, and to her dismay, he kept them all.

At noon, the soldiers ate: rice, omelets, and chicken. (Katy's pet, Jenny, had escaped into the forest.) Nessie approached the lieutenant and signaled she wanted food for Katy. He waved her away, but later sent her food. Al was given nothing, not even water, and was forced to remain standing the long afternoon.

Inside the lean-to, the soldiers guarding Nessie and Dottie began a game of cards. Nessie watched them closely. Once she was familiar with the cards, she asked to have them. They handed her the deck, and she performed a simple card trick, much to their amusement. They motioned to her to repeat it several times until one soldier took the deck from her and performed the trick himself. His companions roared with delight.

At nightfall, Al was untied and allowed to join the women. They were each given a blanket and ordered to crawl under the larger hut to sleep. Al whispered to Nessie that he was sure he was going to be shot when the soldiers tied him to the machine gun.

Later in the afternoon, he made conversation with his guards who knew a little English. He mentioned he had visited Japan, and that there were many Japanese cherry trees in Washington, D.C. The guards told him that the trees had all been chopped down.

Their sleeping place was no bed of roses. Stones and clods of dirt pushed up through the blankets. The guards sleeping above repeatedly shouted at them whenever Katy got fussy. Nevertheless, Al and Nessie slept well that night. The nervous tension they had experienced the week before—worrying about what might be happening in Balbalasang and what might happen to them—had been strangely eased by their capture.

The soldiers woke them before dawn and gave them rice to eat. They were eager to leave for Balbalasang to present their captives to Captain Hirano. They re-tied a rope around Al's waist and gave him two heavy baskets of rice to carry. Nessie and Dottie took turns carrying Katy. The lieutenant led them off at a terrific pace, crossing and re-crossing the river many times before reaching the trail. Al fell repeatedly from the weight of the baskets and the slippery riverbed. Each time he fell, a soldier hit him with the butt of his gun.

Shortly after they started, Nessie realized she needed to urinate, but the soldiers would not let her stray from the path. In desperation, she turned to Dottie and said, "What shall we do?"

"We'll just have to go right here," Dottie replied. And they did, squatting in the path with thirty soldiers as eyewitnesses.

No matter the nature of the terrain, the lieutenant would

march them for fifty minutes, and then rest for ten. Nessie never got any rest, as she had to attend to Katy during the break. She fell when they went up a steep five-hundred-foot incline. When she got to her feet, she fell again. The soldiers took her pack and gave it to one of their *cargadores* to carry. This was a relief to Nessie, but she still couldn't get up the mountain. The soldier in front of her cut a long stick. He held one end. She held the other. The soldier behind her put his hand in the small of her back and shoved. She collapsed in exhaustion when she reached the top of the mountain. A soldier gave her a strong dose of peppermint water, which quickly revived her.

At noon, they stopped for a meal of cold rice and dried fish. Afterwards, the lieutenant set a slower pace, much to Al's and the women's relief.

During rest stops, the soldiers would ask Nessie and Dottie to teach them English words. One took Dottie's crucifix, laughingly bowed and crossed himself, and then refused to give it back to her. Another asked to look through Nessie's glasses. She was afraid he would not return them, but he did. A third soldier pointed to her wedding ring. She had already turned it around so the diamonds would not show. She thought he wanted it, but all he wished to know was the word *ring*.

When they neared Inalangan, just two kilometers from Balbalasang, the lieutenant slowed the pace even more and then called for a long stop so soldiers could help themselves to sugarcane that grew in a nearby field. The soldiers shared a bit with their captives. The lieutenant ordered villagers to march ahead so they could witness the *Padji's* arrival in Balbalasang as a prisoner of the Japanese Imperial Army.

PRISONERS OF THE JAPANESE IMPERIAL ARMY

THE LIEUTENANT LED THEM TO Chief Puyao's house, the largest and most imposing dwelling in the village. Captain Hirano had established it as his headquarters. The lieutenant lined up his captives in front of the steps. Standing in the doorway, Captain Hirano called them to attention at the top of his lungs. Everyone bowed to him.

Nessie began to laugh, much to Al's annoyance. He nudged her in the ribs.

"I can't help it," she said, "I'm not afraid anymore. Hirano reminds me so much of my brother-in-law, Tux."

In his fifties, Captain Hirano had a curved mustache and a paunch, just like Tux. He was rather distinguished looking.

The captain eyed his prisoners carefully, then ordered the lieutenant to take them beneath the house. Like all Tingguian homes, the house was built on stilts high off the ground, so that the space beneath could be used to tether livestock, set up a loom for weaving, or pound rice when it rained. Soldiers had barricaded the space with bamboo and wire. Al, Nessie, and Dottie were surprised to see that beds had been prepared for them. Tied to one of them, to their amazement, was an American with red hair and a beard. Al started to speak to him but he cast Al a warning glance.

Nessie, Katy, and Dottie rested on the beds while Al was led upstairs to Captain Hirano, who sat stiffly behind a desk. Al bowed to him, and the Captain returned the courtesy. Through an interpreter, the Captain ordered Al to write a letter to Chief Puyao. Tell Puyao, Hirano said, that if he surrenders now, his property will be protected and he will not be harmed or imprisoned. He could remain in Balbalasang and help restore law and order. Al wrote the letter. Once it was translated for the Captain, he was led back downstairs.

The fathers of John and Marcus had told Al that the Japanese had burned Puyao's camp at Maatop, which accounted for the ash that had fallen over the forest. The Chief had fled with his wife, two daughters, and the Morrises to the village of Asiga.

When the soldiers began to relax their guard, the redheaded American told Al he had been captured previously, but escaped. He had grown a beard in the hope that the Japanese wouldn't recognize him. They knew him as Captain Hunt, but he was actually a Mr. Harris of the Itogon Mining Company near Baguio.

The small band of prisoners was guarded day and night by ten Japanese soldiers and Philippine Constabulary troops. At six in the evening, the prisoners were ordered to lie flat on their beds and were expected to remain there until six the next morning. A guard stood at the head of each bed. The first night, Katy grew restless because of mosquitoes.

Her restlessness made her want to go to the toilet. When Nessie sat up to take her, she almost got sliced in two by a bayonet. Nessie's sudden movement had startled the guard. He permitted Nessie to take Katy out of the enclosure to squat behind a tree.

A night or two later, when Nessie once again took Katy outside, she noticed Captain Hirano on similar business. He shouted at Nessie at the top of his lungs. She shouted back at the top of hers, "*Kodomo, benjo*"—the only two words she knew in Japanese—"Child, toilet." He smiled pleasantly, buttoned his trousers, and passed her by.

The Japanese kept Al and Captain Hunt tied to their beds day and night. They were able to sit up and walk a few paces. When they needed to answer the call of nature, they would shout "*Benjo,*" and their guards would march them to a screened pit nearby. Villagers eyed the *Padji* sadly when he walked past, led like a dog on a rope.

Nessie and Dottie cooked the meals. The first evening a hard-boiled sergeant gave them rice. They motioned with their hands that they needed cooking utensils, but he paid no attention. Captain Hunt said in a low tone, "Look under my bed." There they found a big pot and a frying pan.

The women split the firewood and cooked over an open fire, setting the pot of rice on three river stones. One evening the soldiers handed Nessie a pig's head. She immediately thrust it into Dottie's hands, "You're the surgeon. I'll be the cook." They couldn't cook the head whole, as they needed the pot for their rice. Dottie scrapped as much meat from the head as she could, and they fried that. Another evening, the sergeant handed Nessie the underskin of a sow's belly, with teats. She started to laugh. Holding up the underskin for the others to see, she laughed so hard the tears rolled down her face. She just couldn't stop. She and Dottie did their best to make this "select cut" palatable.

Occasionally, a villager would come up to the enclosure with an egg for Katy. The soldier on guard always gave it to her.

A few days after their capture, Captain Hirano gave his captives permission to go to the Saltan River to bathe. Guards led Al and Captain Hunt to the river by their ropes, while a guard followed closely behind Nessie, Katy, and Dottie. The women noticed that the lieutenant was swimming in their favorite swimming hole, while further downstream many of the soldiers were bathing nude. Al and Captain Hunt were led further upstream. The women's guard ordered them to stay put. He squatted on the pebbly beach to watch them.

"What shall we do, Nessie?" said Dottie.

"Why, I am going to take a bath," Nessie replied. And she did, and so too did Dottie. Nessie scrubbed Katy, and they pounded the dirty clothes they had removed. They relished being clean again and feeling the warm sunlight on their skin.

Every day Captain Hirano and his men made great demands on the villagers, eating their rice, butchering their pigs and carabaos, and drinking their *basi* (rice wine). When two weeks passed and Chief Puyao still had not surrendered, an angry and impatient Captain Hirano ordered that the Chief's house be burned. His soldiers quickly escorted their captives outside and removed tables, chairs, and beds before setting the house ablaze. Flames crackled, smoke billowed above the coconut trees, villagers shouted and wept. The Chief's house was reduced to ashes in minutes.

Captain Hirano marched over to his captives and announced he was sending them the next day, along with hostage members of Chief Puyao's family, to Bontoc, the capital of the Mountain Province. There the *Padji* would stand trial.

Trek to Lubuagan

AT DAWN, RAIN WAS COMING DOWN in sheets. The guards told Nessie and Dottie to prepare breakfast. The women squatted by the open fire, trying to shelter the small flame from the rain and pushing in pieces of pine pitch to keep it going. Perhaps emboldened by his anger at the burning of Chief Puyao's house, a villager handed each of the women an umbrella.

After breakfast, when it stopped raining, everyone— prisoners, soldiers, hostages, and *cargadores*—were ordered to line up. In all, the group numbered about a hundred. Captain Hunt was ordered to the head of the line, followed by soldiers, Al, more soldiers, *cargadores*, hostages, and finally Nessie, Katy, and Dottie. Captain Hirano looked them over carefully, then announced that he would remain behind to capture Chief Puyao.

Nessie had begun menstruating. When the soldiers ordered her to carry Katy, she told them she did not have the strength. The soldiers insisted that if she didn't carry Katy, she would have to carry a heavy load instead. She still refused. Captain Hunt intervened on her behalf and told the soldiers that she was ill and would not be able to carry anything. The soldiers handed her a *pasiking* that contained their cooking pots. It weighed only ten pounds.

She was able to carry it, but still found the going difficult because she was so weak. Each time the soldiers stopped for a rest, Nessie pulled off to the side of the trail to attend to herself. She was grateful she was at the end of the line, but a soldier always stayed by her and watched the entire performance. She could not dispose of the cloth she was using because she had no more. She washed it in irrigation ditches along the way.

At noon, they reached the village of Pantikian. Al hoped they would stop for food, but the soldiers marched them straight through the village for another kilometer before calling a halt for rest. Villagers brought them food— rice, chicken, and vegetables. The soldiers gave Al and Captain Hunt only rice. Aware of this, Nessie brought the two men chicken. While the lieutenant allowed her to give some to Al, he would not let her approach Captain Hunt.

Resuming their twenty-six kilometer trek, they reached the village of Salegseg late in the afternoon. Soldiers led them to a public school building where they would spend the night. Al and Captain Hunt were ordered inside while Nessie was handed five empty pots and told to fetch water. A Philippine Constabulary guard accompanied her to the Saltan River. Along the way, village women tried to talk to her, but she didn't trust her guard. Beyond saying the people of Balbalasang were all right, she kept silent.

At the river, Nessie filled the five pots with water. They were heavy and awkward to carry, and she was grateful when her guard offered to carry two of them. But when they got near the school, he handed them back to her, and she had to juggle all five.

At four the next morning, the soldiers woke their prisoners and hostages. Once again, they ordered Nessie and Dottie to cook—and handed them an old wooden school desk to use as firewood. But they didn't give them a machete to chop it with. Nessie and Dottie eyed each other and stood still, refusing to budge when soldiers urged them to get busy. Perhaps tired of the game, one soldier finally handed Nessie a bunch of lighted *runo* to start the fire. Then he broke up the desk for them.

Once again, they trekked all day, reaching the small village of Ableg on the banks of the Pasil River at nightfall. Soldiers ordered villagers to share their homes with them. Captain Hunt, Dottie, Al, Nessie, and Katy were assigned the same house. Filthy from two days of hiking, they used a small basin to wash off some of their grime. Al and Captain Hunt had developed huge blisters on their heels, and one of the soldiers treated them. He threaded a large needle with a coarse thread, punctured each blister, and pulled the thread all the way through the blister.

Nessie and Dottie prepared dinner from some meat and green papayas soldiers had given them. Afterwards, their host, the owner of the house, shared some *basi* with them. The *basi* tasted a bit like apple cider, and they found it cool and refreshing.

The next morning, they set out on the last stretch of their trip to Lubuagan. Earlier in the war, to slow the

Japanese advance, guerrillas had dynamited the bridge across the Pasil River. Soldiers led their captives and hostages along the edge of rice fields to a steep incline above the river. They slid down the incline, crossed the river at that point, then hiked up an even steeper incline to reach more rice fields and, finally, the road. Waiting for them there were several trucks loaded with soldiers. Al suspected the soldiers were on their way to round up other Americans in Kalinga.

The lieutenant ordered his captives and hostages into one of the trucks soldiers had vacated. They had to squeeze tightly together to make room, but were grateful they did not have to hike the remaining eleven kilometers to Lubuagan. Throughout the ride, one of Chief Puyao's daughters sat with her head in Nessie's lap weeping. Nessie tried to comfort her. All she could think to say was that she was sure everything would be all right.

They were driven to the Kalinga Academy compound, which the Japanese garrison in Lubuagan used as headquarters. The officers on duty greeted them coldly and led them to a room on the second floor. On the way up, they saw Sergeant Meratio, who had spent Christmas with them at Maatop. Meratio was being slapped by a soldier. After they were given a small amount of rice to eat, Al was led downstairs for questioning.

Through an interpreter, the interrogating officer emphasized that it was very important for Al to tell the truth. He told Al to look under his desk. "There," he pointed, "are all your diaries." Al smiled to himself. The "diaries" were Dottie's five books of devotion, taken from her when they were captured.

The officer asked Al where Major Cushing was hiding. Al replied that he had heard Cushing had been killed in an ambush in the Cagayan Valley. Surely, the officer already knew this, Al thought. The officer dropped that line of questioning, then scolded Al for being a hypocrite—for choosing to fight the Japanese when he was a priest. Now, he said almost casually, Al would have to suffer the consequences.

Dottie and Nessie were also interrogated, but were only asked biographical information.

At sunset, the captives and hostages were given the usual order to "Go Sleepee." They needed no order. They were exhausted from their three-day journey and were soon fast asleep on the hard floor. But a soldier woke them up. From the smell of his breath, Al knew he was drunk. The soldier held a small paper bag above them and kept repeating, "*Kodomo! Kodomo!*" (child). Nessie took the bag. Inside were a few pieces of candy. Nessie and Al bowed to him and said "*Arrigato*" (thank-you). Using sign language, the soldier told them he had three small children in Tokyo.

Dottie went outside to the toilet. She was laughing when she returned. When she had entered, a soldier was sitting on one vacancy. She started to back out, but he motioned her to it—and handed her a roll of toilet paper. She sat.

Death Sentence

THEY ARRIVED IN BONTOC THE NEXT DAY, after a forty-kilometer ride in the back of a truck on a twisting, narrow road that wound in and out of sheer cliffs that fell straight down to the Chico River, several hundred feet below. Around each turn, they held their breath.

When the truck pulled into the Japanese garrison, a very ill tempered officer greeted them. He looked directly at Al and said, "Are you Father Griffiths?"

"Yes, sir," Al replied.

"You're not a good person. You fought the Japanese and killed many at Lamonan."

"No, I didn't fight the Japanese at Lamonan," Al said, truthfully.

While the hostages were led away, the officer ushered Al and the women into a small room. There they sat on benches, wondering what would come next. An hour later, they were each given a plate of rice. One of the guards blew up a red balloon and gave it to Katy, to her delight. The afternoon wore on. Al and Nessie grew more and more tense.

Suddenly they heard the clicking of heels. Guards snapped to attention and ordered them to rise as Colonel Watanabe entered the room. Immaculately dressed in his officer's uniform, the Colonel stood erect, and glared at Al as if he were the devil himself. Al bowed to him, but the Colonel did not return the courtesy. He took a seat behind a desk, ordered his interpreter to stand next to him, and brusquely motioned the women to sit.

The Colonel pointed to Al and snapped, "You are a priest of the Church. You are the *worst* American in Kalinga. Why did you hide in the mountains so long?"

"I was frightened," said Al.

"Frightened? Why were you frightened? Japanese are good people."

"I found a flyer that said I must surrender before June first or I would be killed. I had a bad leg infection. My leg healed after June first."

"You hate us. Why is that?"

"No, I do not hate the Japanese."

"You gave speeches urging the Tingguian people to hate the Japanese."

"I do not hate the Japanese. When I was a youth, I gave money to help rebuild Tokyo after the 1923 earthquake. My father gave much money also."

Colonel Watanabe pounded his fist on the desk, interrupting the interpreter. He handed a letter to Al.

It was from Bishop Binsted in Manila, urging him to surrender.

"I never received this letter," Al said. "If I had, I would have surrendered immediately. I'm a priest, and I must obey my Bishop."

"Instead you joined the guerrillas."

Al replied that he had been a reserve chaplain before the war began.

The colonel rose slowly and deliberately, anger rising in his face. In one quick breath, he said to Al, "You will be executed." Then he left the room.

Al had no reaction when he heard the pronouncement. He felt no emotion. But Nessie shouted at the colonel that if he killed Al, he could kill her too.

The ill-tempered officer who had greeted them on their arrival returned and waved a paper he had taken from Al in his face. It proved Al was a guerrilla, he said, because it bore Major Cushing's signature. The signature was not Cushing's, Al countered, but the Chief of Chaplains' signature. The document commissioned him as a chaplain. Furthermore, it had been signed on July 6, 1941, six months before the start of the war. Al felt exhausted and depressed. Would this clarification save his life?

Soldiers took Al and the women to a large brick building that served as a prison. There, they were led to a small jail cell that held a Filipino and two captured American soldiers, including a Lieutenant Taulbee who gave Nessie a bar of soap to clean Katy. Later that evening three Chinese men were shoved in with them.

Their dinner consisted of a little rice and Chinese cabbage served in a garbage can. The cabbage looked so filthy that Nessie, Katy, and Dottie wouldn't eat it. But the men did and they suffered miserably from diarrhea that night. Their guard refused to allow anyone out of the cell long enough to relieve himself in the open-pit toilet a few meters away. Instead, the men had to use a pot just outside the cell.

Each morning for two days, the men were taken outside, given shovels, and ordered to dig trenches. After supper on the second day, the routine was broken. The men were ordered back to work. Each was given a shovel except Al. Had the time come for his execution, he wondered. Had the other men been given shovels to dig his grave? Meanwhile, Nessie and Dottie waited breathlessly in their prison cell but heard no shots fired. What they could not see was that Al had been given a machete to cut palm fronds to camouflage the trenches.[15]

---

[15] The description of this event is slightly different from Al's recollection on camera (see Prologue). In the on-camera interview, he may have been referring to his initial reaction when Japanese soldiers handed him a shovel the first day of his imprisonment in Bontoc. What is described here occurred at the end of his second day of imprisonment in Bontoc.

REPRIEVE

THE NEXT MORNING all the captives received the very welcome news that they would be taken to Baguio. Once they were on their way, jammed into the back of a truck, Al breathed a huge sigh of relief. He was sure this meant he was not going to be executed. On the road to Baguio—with its expansive mountain scenery—even their guards seemed happy. They asked their captives to sing, and sing they did, two of Al's favorites: "Oh, Susannah" and "Alouette," plus many others. Singing was such a release. Al and Nessie felt that nothing could be worse than what they had just been through.

Upon their arrival in Baguio hours later, the prisoners were driven to the Military Police Building at Camp John Hay and ordered to remain outside on the grass. Soldiers and officers came out of the building to stare at them, and a few gave Katy some candy. The prisoners were a sight to behold. Al and Captain Hunt had long hair and beards. Al's hair had turned completely gray during his months in the forest. He looked more like an old man than a 37-year-old. Nessie had on a shirt and a pair of slacks she had sewn at Maatop at Christmas using her brightly flowered cretonne curtains that a villager had kept for her. Ever the Britisher, Dottie was the tidiest of the bunch, her long hair tied neatly in a net, a white nurse's apron protecting her light blue blouse and skirt.

Soldiers ordered the prisoners to the firehouse, a short walk away, and lined them up in front of the building. To Al and Nessie's surprise, out walked an American, Captain Perryam, whom they had last seen at Maatop on Christmas Day. Before the soldiers could stop him, Al walked up to Perryam, shook his hand, and whispered that he must not identify Hunt. Perryam identified Al as a priest, Nessie and Dottie as missionaries, and Meratio as one of his soldiers. He disclaimed knowledge of Hunt and the others.

Soldiers led Nessie, Katy, and Dottie into a side room of the firehouse, where they joined a Filipino woman with her husband and three children. The other men were kept in the main room. For the first time since being captured, Al and Hunt had their ropes removed. Later in the afternoon, they were permitted to go to the mess hall—some fifty meters away—to pick up rations of rice and mixed vegetables. Al was allowed to take Katy with him, and she enjoyed the freedom as much as the men did. An American soldier whom the Japanese were using as a truck driver came running up to her, saying she was the first American child he had seen since the war started—and that he had children of his own back in the States.

The next morning, April 11, Palm Sunday 1943, a young, somewhat brash, Japanese soldier entered the fire station and yelled, "Hello, folks! Anybody here from Cal?"

Meratio answered, "I'm from Santa Monica."

"Hell," the soldier replied, "I graduated from San Diego High School."

He then announced that military prisoners would be sent to Cabanatuan prison and civilians to Camp Holmes. Al held his breath, fearing he would be sent to Cabanatuan because of his guerrilla activity. He relaxed when he was ordered to Camp Holmes with the women. The military prisoners—Captain Perryam, Sergeant Meratio, and others—were lined up in pairs, then tied to one another to prevent them from running away.

Al, Nessie, Katy, and Dottie were ordered into the back of an armored truck and driven around Baguio for public display. They didn't mind, for some of their Filipino friends saw them, including one young man from Balbalasang. For some months after their internment, their friends sent them bags of food. Finally, the truck headed for Camp Holmes, a former Philippine Constabulary camp, set on a pine-forested hillside a few miles north of Baguio. As they pulled into the camp, they could hear the voices of a large number of people celebrating Palm Sunday services in the amphitheater. With its green parade grounds and distant view of the South China Sea, Camp Holmes seemed like a haven to Al, Nessie, and Dottie.

The prisoners were taken to the main office and met by Japanese officers and Miss Spencer, an internee who had served as a missionary in Japan. She spoke Japanese and interpreted for the officer who had accompanied them from Camp John Hay.

"He asks me to tell you," Miss Spencer said to Al, "that he knows you are a military man. But because you have a family, he is making a special concession and permitting you to enter Camp Holmes."

"Please tell the officer," said Al, "that I deeply appreciate his decision."

They bowed politely to the officer, picked up their few belongings, and made their way to the camp's barracks where old friends greeted them warmly. It was sixteen months into the war.

Al, Nessie, and Dottie did not tell their friends about Al's participation in the guerrilla movement. They kept it secret, both to protect themselves and their American friends still in hiding.

PRISON CAMP LIFE

AL, NESSIE, KATY, AND DOTTIE were among the last Americans in the Philippines to be interned. The five hundred other internees at Camp Holmes, mostly miners and missionaries, plus all the students and faculty of Brent School in Baguio, had been imprisoned for more than a year. Many had been allowed to enter camp with their personal possessions—clothes, blankets, books, extra food stores—but Al, Nessie, and Katy entered camp with only one change of clothes and a blanket each, plus the twenty dollars Captain Perryam had given Al at Christmas.

Natalie Crouter, in her book, *Forbidden Diary*, records their arrival:

> ....the three Griffiths and Miss Taverner, from the mountains, were held two weeks before coming here and were told to send out for their household goods, which they had dispersed with Igorot friends. These were sent in—then confiscated as property of the Army because they had hidden out so long. Even the rings were taken off their fingers, wedding ring included. Mr. Griffiths was tied to a wall with a rope around his waist. We feel worn out with fury and disturbance.[16]

---

[16] Crouter, Natalie, *Forbidden Diary*, p. 154.

Al, Nessie, and Dottie quickly incorporated into camp routine. It was a sharp contrast to their unstructured life in the forest. The camp commandant, Major Rokuro Tomibe, had allowed the internees to organize themselves and they did so aggressively. The Men's Committee established camp policy, determining such things as the allocation of food and supplies. Women had their own committee, which made recommendations to the Men's Committee.

Both committees were assigned work. Men cut firewood and ran the machine shop, while women served as waiters and did the camp laundry. Both men and women taught at the camp school and worked in the camp hospital. Among the internees were ten doctors and thirty-two nurses.[17] Dottie added to their ranks. Al and Nessie were assigned kitchen duties.

For an hour-and-a-half every morning, Nessie worked in the vegetable room. She had her potato peeler, which she used when hiding out. The peeler made her doubly useful because she could peel vegetables faster than the knife-wielders, and she wasted less. But Nessie noticed the peeler caused some hard feelings since she got the best vegetables to work on, and one day it disappeared.

Months later, when the camp diet had begun to take its toll on her health, Nessie grew too weak to move her arm continuously even for that short period. She asked to be

---

[17] Bloom, Lynn Z., *Forbidden Diary* by Natalie Crouter, Introduction, p. xx.

transferred to the rice table where she picked out tiny white worms from the grain.

Al was assigned the job of dishwasher. But when Alex, the chief cook—once the chef at an elite Hong Kong Hotel—learned that Al and Nessie had spent their honeymoon in Hong Kong, he immediately promoted Al to assistant cook. The high point of Al's career came one night when he asked Alex to let him make fish cakes instead of serving the routine boiled rice and fish. After some argument, Alex gave his hesitant consent—on the understanding that Al would take full responsibility not only for the cakes but for the wrath that was sure to descend on the heads of the kitchen crew when the meal was served. But to Alex's surprise—and Al's relief—the fish cakes were a big success, and they became a standard item on the menu.

Until the last three months of the war, the Japanese command provided internees with three meals a day. According to Bloom, internees received "the basic Japanese Army ration, a peasant-diet of low-quality food, consisting of vegetables and staples." [18]

Once when a member of the garbage crew was ill, Al took his place. Being on the garbage crew was a choice assignment for it meant getting outside the camp gates. Al went off with Katy in tow. When they returned, Katy held in her hand a precious egg—and a gardenia for Nessie. Al held a glass jar, which contained a polliwog he had caught

[18] Ibid.

for Katy. Nessie placed the jar on the windowsill above where she and Katy slept on the floor. Each day Katy fed her pet polliwog fresh nasturtium leaves.

Al and Nessie were unaware when they were assigned their jobs that, within the camp social hierarchy, the cook and kitchen crew, according to Bloom, "ranked among the elite because of their constant proximity to food, with its advantages of extra nourishment and opportunities for graft." Bloom says pre-war status was "irrelevant in camp" and that hierarchy was "based on a new set of values."

Highest in the camp hierarchy were the translator Nellie McKim, and the head of the Men's Committee, Elmer Herold. Nellie had been raised in Japan, spoke Japanese, and was well acquainted with Japanese culture. Elmer had employed many Japanese before the war at his logging company outside Baguio. On behalf of the internees, both were effective in establishing positive relationships with their captors.

The Roman Catholic priest, Fr. Sheridan, was also much respected—and beloved. He had voluntarily interned himself so the Catholics in camp would have a priest.

Men and women lived in separate dormitories, with boys twelve and older sleeping with their fathers in the men's dormitory, and younger children with their mothers in the women's dormitory. Single women, including girls twelve and older, lived in a third dormitory. Because space was at a premium, every adult was allotted a space just thirty-three inches wide, a bit less for each child.[19]

In addition to the dormitories, the camp had an infirmary (where a clandestine radio was hidden), a school, a workshop, and animal sheds where internees kept pigs, goats, and chickens. It also had a large parade ground—the site of many a softball game, and a cemetery on the hill above the camp where internees who died were buried.

Missionary friends gave Al and Nessie clothes to augment their meager wardrobe. Al also received some clothes from camp welfare. Internees with clothing they no longer had use for turned it in to the camp welfare room. The clothing was then distributed to those in need.

Nessie made pants for Katy with material a friend gave her, and she also made Katy a blouse and skirt with a blue-and-white scarf a clergyman gave her. Katy was wearing this outfit one day when a guard stopped her as she was crossing the parade ground with nasturtiums she had picked for her polliwog. The guard took her picture and later gave Al and Nessie a copy of it, the only picture taken of Katy between the ages of two and five.

The Sisters of St. Anne, an order of Episcopal nuns, had come into camp with huge quantities of colored string. They gave some of it to Nessie, and she used it to knit Katy a sweater and a red-and-white skirt, plus underwear and several pairs of socks, all very durable.

---

[19] Ibid, p. xxiii.

Nessie's hobnail boots weren't very popular with her dormitory mates who found them too noisy. When a neighbor offered Nessie a pair of blue tennis shoes, she accepted them graciously and wore them for weeks—until the fatal day her the neighbor's little girl knocked Katy's polliwog out the window to the sidewalk below.

The incident left both women on edge. A short while later, when Nessie heard her neighbor remark about Nessie's lack of gratitude for the shoes on her feet, Nessie—in a rather high-handed tone of voice she later regretted—returned them to her. Nessie went barefoot until the men in the machine shop made her a pair of wooden clogs. It took a while for her to get used to them, but when the blisters healed and the calluses developed, she discovered they were very serviceable, especially in rainy weather.

Bloom writes, "By the time the captives were liberated in February 1945, they—as well as their captors—were suffering from severe malnutrition." [20] Nevertheless, only twelve internees died during the war and, according to Bloom, most of those died of old age or pre-existing infirmities. She writes:

> One explanation for this striking phenomenon is that the integrity of the captives' individual personalities was not destroyed. The internees did not lapse into passivity or childlike dependence on their captors... Indeed, the resourcefulness and ingenuity they had exhibited in their pre-war occupations—as missionaries

[20] Ibid, p. xxiv.

(members of twenty-two sects were in camp), business people, and mining engineers—enabled them to adapt well to new conditions and to prevail over them as fully as possible. The internees maintained a strong, life-preserving sense of their identities, and their solidarity as members of functioning, purposeful groups, despite individual disagreements. Although there were emotional fluctuations, the prevailing mood among the internees was resigned and determined optimism.[21]

[21] Ibid.

A BOON FROM THE RED CROSS

INITIALLY, AL AND NESSIE WERE THRILLED with the variety of vegetables served at camp meals, especially after the limitations of their diet in the forest, but they soon learned to keep their comments to themselves. Fellow internees, who had already been imprisoned for a year, did not view the menus with favor, and, in time, even Al and Nessie found the regular mixture of boiled vegetables unappealing.

For the first few months of their captivity, every other week they were fortunate to receive a paper bag, dropped at the camp gate, that contained papayas, bananas, eggs, and on one never-to-be-forgotten occasion, strawberries. They never learned who sent them the food. The fictitious name on the bag gave them no clue. Eventually, the camp commandant prohibited internees from receiving such gifts. Then their diet became very slim.

When times grew tougher than usual, they would spend a little of their twenty-dollar nest egg at the camp store, usually for a few eggs for Katy, or a few bananas for all of them. As Nessie was shopping at the store one day, she noticed that the cashier pushed an additional tiny bunch of bananas toward her as she reached for her small purchase. Thinking he had made a mistake, she pushed them back, not realizing he was trying to do her a favor.

Friendly Seventh Day Adventists who had gotten into camp with their goats, mattresses, and cooking utensils, lent Nessie pans and plates until she was able to collect a few tins of her own. Many of their fellow Episcopal missionaries had a supply of canned goods, and they occasionally invited Al, Nessie, Katy, and Dottie to a meal.

Nessie did not hesitate to take advantage whenever an opportunity for extra food came her way. One afternoon, she noticed a miner's wife cooking dozens of cookies—and shoving to the side all the burnt ones. Nessie asked her what she was going to do with them.

"Why," the woman answered, "I'm going to throw them out."

"In that case, may I have them?" Nessie inquired.

For three days running she, Al, and Katy had burnt cookies for evening dessert.

Another time, Nessie noticed her next-door neighbor in the dormitory was about to dispose of some wormy *bucacao*, a grain similar to kafir corn, so she asked her for it. Nessie washed the *bucacao* many times, dried it thoroughly, and then tried to pop it like popcorn. To her great delight, it popped. She sealed it in an airtight tin and gave Katy some when she got hungry or when they celebrated a birthday or anniversary.

But the best food event of all was the arrival of Red Cross food boxes for Christmas 1943, the first—and only—Red Cross boxes to reach Camp Holmes. Each contained pounds of powdered milk, raisins, prunes, packages of

American cheese, tins of Spam, canned ham and eggs, butter, chocolate, and cartons of cigarettes. Some internees ate the content of their boxes within a few weeks. Others planned to stretch theirs over a year. Al and Nessie decided to make their box last six months. As it turned out, they managed to stretch their Red Cross supplies for fourteen months.

Because single men were anxious to have cigarettes, Al traded most of his for cans of powdered milk for Katy. Al and Nessie used none of it for themselves until a year later when Al came down with a severe case of dengue fever and could not keep anything down.

The cigarettes that Al didn't trade he smuggled out to American soldiers still hiding in the mountains. He and Nessie also sent out tins of meat and string socks Nessie had knitted. Whenever they indulged in a tin of meat inside the barbed wire fence, they hoped soldiers outside were also having a taste.

In addition to the food boxes, the Camp Holmes internees also received a windfall of clothing in an allotment from the Red Cross. The problem was how to distribute it fairly. One person receiving more than another would have been a catastrophe. With the approval of the Men's Committee, an internee with a background in social science devised a numerical system by which each person made out three lists of preferences. If someone didn't get his or her first choice, he or she would get their second or third. Al and Nessie made their lists identical—and as a result got the articles they most desired. At the top of their list were shoes for all of them, a wool coat for Katy, underwear for Al, and a playsuit and nightgown for Nessie. Everyone received towels, sheets, and soap. Nessie traded one of their sheets for another playsuit.

UNEXPECTED VISITORS

EVEN UNDER THE MOST ADVERSE CIRCUMSTANCES, Americans can have a good time. The Camp Holmes internees were no exception. Every afternoon, except during the worst days of the rainy season, men and boys would play softball on the parade ground while the women and children watched from the sidelines and cheered them on. Until the men and boys grew too weak to play, these games were the internees' favorite form of entertainment.

In the evening, many internees played bridge. Fridays were designated as tournament night and Al and Nessie discovered that their game improved greatly. They were in the semi-finals in one tournament and came out on top in another.

Internees also held dances until the day came when they didn't have the strength to cavort. They also had bi-monthly educational programs. Missionaries and priests gave lectures on theology. Miners gave talks on geology. The resident anthropologist, Roy F. Barton, presented a series of lectures on the society and culture of Philippine mountain tribal groups. Talent shows were also popular. Nessie danced the hula at one. Activities were reported in a camp newspaper by a young journalist, James Halsema.

Katy Griffiths in Camp Holmes Internment Camp. She is wearing a blouse and skirt made from a bureau scarf and carrying nasturtium leaves to feed her pet polliwog. A Japanese prison guard took the photo and gave it to Nessie.

But the recreation that gave Al and Nessie the most pleasure was accorded by the Camp Commandant, Major Rokuro Tomibe, who announced one day that internees could have private gardens. In his hours away from the kitchen, Al worked hard on his small garden plot. For both him and Nessie, going to their garden was like a tiny vacation, allowing them respite from the noise and confusion of camp. Al grew onions, peppers, cabbage, and celery in his small plot, and he even produced enough celery to provide the whole camp with a ration.

Major Tomibe also permitted internees to take picnic lunches up into the pine-forested hills above the camp. Going into the hills was like entering another world. Al and Nessie could be affectionate with each other. They could talk above a whisper without being overheard. Best of all, they could relax.

Dottie often accompanied them on these excursions, and it wasn't long before they had a few favorite spots. Nessie would prepare a picnic lunch of thick pancakes (made of rice flour, powdered milk, and a little treasured fat) and a small tin of canned ham from their Red Cross rations, which she divided into four portions, affording each of them about a tablespoon or two of meat. Sometimes there would be an egg to divide and, while their Red Cross supplies were most plentiful, they would have raisins and a bit of chocolate for dessert. Afterwards they would lie on their backs in the grass while Katy colored a picture or made a little "garden."

But good things come to an end, and so did this privilege when two men walked off one day and did not return. Both were Army men who chose to rejoin the guerrillas. Their escape proved to be tough on their best friends in camp as well as the other internees. Two of their closest friends, and the young newspaperman, James Halsema, were taken out of camp and tortured for several days until they revealed what they knew. The wives of the two friends who were tortured remained stoic throughout the ordeal. The whole camp rejoiced with them when their husbands, as well as Halsema, finally returned, worse for their experiences but still alive.

Major Tomibe was immediately removed from his position as commandant. He was essentially a kind man and had treated internees gently. Though not a Christian himself, his wife had attended the Episcopal Church school in Kyoto, and he had known a number of American missionaries prior to the onset of the war.

Taking his place was Major Oura. Bowing came into style. Male internees were required to guard all the dormitories and patrol through them every hour of the night. The patrolling gradually ended, but each internee still had to be checked in at bedtime. Fr. Sheridan was given that responsibility and he recruited Nessie to help him.

One day not long after the two internees escaped, a car unexpectedly drove in to camp. With much shouting and snapping to attention at the guardhouse, Al and Nessie knew someone of importance had arrived. They walked over to see what the fuss was about and were startled when an officer sprang up from his seat, shouted, and motioned for them to approach. It was Captain Hirano. He greeted them like long-lost friends. Next to him—but remaining seated—was Colonel Watanabe. He offered them a frosty smile without speaking when they bowed.

The next day, Al and Nessie were even more surprised when they received another unexpected visitor, Kazuo Fujihara, one of their captors. He had come expressly to see Katy. He had been very kind to her, allowing her to accept eggs from villagers, and picking wild strawberries for her on the long trek from Balbalasang to Lubuagan. Al and Nessie conversed with him for some time through their interpreter, Miss Spencer. Before he departed, he said he would like to leave a little gift for Katy. He had meant to bring her milk but could not buy any. Would Nessie accept a small gift of money to buy her extra food? Nessie hesitated for a moment, wondering what her fellow internees might think, and then accepted the gift in the spirit in which it was offered. With it, she bought Katy three eggs at the camp store.

CHRISTMAS 1943

AT FIRST, KATY HAD BEEN OVERWHELMED by camp life. After sixteen months in the forest, seeing only few Balbalasang men and no children (except for Christmas at Ma-atop), she was stunned by the confusion, noise, and sheer numbers of children in camp, rarely venturing far from the side of Al or Nessie. She had turned two years old shortly after Pearl Harbor, and was four when captured. She eventually acquired playmates, but she didn't adjust well to the camp's kindergarten class, and Nessie didn't insist she attend.

Nessie did not regret this decision until the day the Japanese guards presented a program for the schoolchildren. Nessie inquired if Katy might go, but was informed by one of the kindergarten teachers that she wasn't invited. What hurt Nessie the most was not the attitude of the teacher—although that rankled a bit—but the fact that the guards gave each child two bananas at the conclusion of the program.

During their months in the forest, Al and Nessie entertained Katy as best as they could. With Dottie's deck of miniature cards, Katy had learned to recognize numbers and to count. She committed to memory her entire book of Mother Goose rhymes, and Al and Nessie taught her all the poetry they themselves could remember, including selections from Robert Louis Stevenson's *Child's Garden of Verses*. She knew her alphabet and could sing a large number of songs and hymns with stories, including "My Old Kentucky Home," and "Jesus Bides Us Shine with a Clean Pure Light."

Katy enrolled in kindergarten during their second year of captivity, and she loved it. At the end of the year, she was issued a certificate. It read, "Awarded to Katharine Clark Griffiths on completion of the Camp Holmes Kindergarten, 1944," and was signed by the principal of the lower school and by Elmer Herold, Chairman of the Men's Committee. On the certificate was painted a kitten dressed in a flower-sprigged skirt with a bow of yellow around its head and a blue book in its hand.

Parents tried to make Christmas and birthdays as special as they could for their children. Katy's birthday came just two weeks before Christmas, so Al and Nessie planned a double celebration for Christmas 1943. They invited twenty-six children to a party for her. They had saved for weeks in preparation. Nessie made crackers out of cassava flour, juice, and fruit salad (with fruit she and Al had received from their unknown friend outside camp). She also made a cake from cassava flour, brown sugar, an egg, and lard.

Van Wie Bergamini, the Episcopal Mission's architect, built Katy a ship out of a five-gallon gasoline tin. Al placed it in the center of the table, and Nessie surrounded it with sunflowers that grew wild in the hills above the camp. Katy was so excited when she saw the table and all her guests that she ran from one end of the long dining room to the other and back again before Al and Nessie could get her to calm down. Each child had brought her a little gift, including an egg beautifully painted by an English woman from Hong Kong, a pencil, a papaya, and even three tiny tomatoes in a small paper sack.

For Christmas, Nessie made Katy a doll using a pattern that a fellow internee gave her. She embroidered the face with floss she begged from kindly neighbors, stuffed the body with stuffing from another neighbor's mattress, and sewed on wool hair raveled from a light-colored sweater still another neighbor gave her. The wool was curly so the doll had a very definite permanent wave. Nessie made the doll's dress from a dancing frock that an instructor had brought into camp. The dress was a peach color and had big ruffles and a blue satin bow. Dottie crocheted a peach-and-blue-colored hat to tilt saucily on one side of the doll's head. Nessie was very proud of her accomplishment, and Katy was delighted with her special Christmas present.

The Japanese command permitted internees to have their Christmas dinner, picnic-style on the parade ground. The rainy season had ended, and the day was bright, clear, and just a bit cool. In addition to themselves and Katy, Al and Nessie's picnic group comprised those who had hid out in the mountains of Kalinga and Abra: Dottie, and Dolly Morris and her two children, Denis and Garnett, Jr. The Morrises had been captured just a few weeks after Al and

Nessie. Unfortunately, the Japanese separated Garnett from his family and sent him to Cabanatuan, a military prison, along with four other men they had captured at the same time. Despite their circumstances, everyone in the group had a wonderful Christmas, united by their common bond.

But just a few weeks later, Dolly Morris died suddenly. She was ironing clothes one afternoon when she collapsed from a heart attack. She was gone before anyone could come to her assistance.

Al conducted the funeral service in the school building where all the church services were held. A number of parents expressed dismay that Nessie and Dottie took Denis and Katy to the service. But both the children were familiar with death and they did as they would have done in Balbalasang—attended the service and carried little bouquets of flowers to place on the grave. Nessie and Dottie both felt it would have been beyond Denis's understanding had they kept her from going. Attending the funeral was the last thing Denis could do for her mother, and she did it well. Dolly's neighbor in camp assumed responsibility for the two Morris children.

CUBICLE WAR

BY 1944, THE THIRD YEAR OF INTERNMENT for most of the internees at Camp Holmes, food allotments had dropped, and internees became much weaker. Those with young children, such as Nessie, found it difficult to care for themselves and their youngsters. They needed help, so they made a daring request—that their husbands move in with them.

Nessie's allotted floor space in her dormitory was sixteen feet in length and slightly less than six feet in width. After a few weeks in camp, she had been provided with a three-quarter-size bed for herself and Katy—their sole piece of furniture until Al built them a tiny table with three little stools. Al had a smaller space in the men's dormitory where he was surrounded by Lutheran ministers. Their theological discussions ranged far into the night.

In making the request for their husbands to move in with them, the women's minds were not on sex. By this point, their low-calorie diet had left them almost devoid of interest in it. The women with young children simply needed their husbands to help care for them, to carry them when needed, to bathe and dress them. But the single women saw in their request only the desire for sexual relations. On that mistaken assumption, they waged a bitter

CUBICLE WAR

war. They argued that food was too scarce to give women who became pregnant extra rations—nor could the camp provide extra milk for the babies that surely would be born.

Soon the discussions went beyond the bounds of respectability, and somber-minded churchgoers were not speaking to one another. The Roman Catholic priest Fr. Sheridan was in favor of his families being together, as were most of the Protestants. But Episcopalians were sharply divided on the issue. Only Al and Nessie and one other Episcopal family favored the proposal, which internees dubbed "the cubicle plan." While the other family argued its case, Al and Nessie chose not to. The single women circulated a petition against the plan. Even the Sisters of St. Anne signed it.

At the height of the battle, Nessie was crossing the parade ground one afternoon when a Sister of St. Anne approached her and said, "Mrs. Griffiths, please just let me ask you one question. Why do you and Father Griffiths favor the cubicle plan?"

Nessie stopped, looked her straight in the eye, and said, "Sister, to us marriage is a sacrament."

The plan was put to a vote, those in favor won, and husbands quickly and joyfully moved in with their wives.

Space was carefully measured. Nessie rated the width of one more board, and an additional four inches. Carpentry was in full swing. Al added an upper bunk to Nessie's bed for Katy and built three shelves at the end of the bed for Nessie's cooking cans and enamel plates. Great was the

135

noise as other men also built small additions to their cubicles. And great was the change when all the sheets and blankets anyone could spare were hung so that each cubicle became a tiny private haven.

For a few days, life in the dormitory was hectic. Couples had to look twice to make sure they were entering their own cubicles. And the women had to get used to the men's heavy boots and the sounds of their snoring. But they all enjoyed the privacy. Al and Nessie could ask two friends in to play bridge without having the whole dormitory watch them. Everyone could escape the ever-present feeling of being reproved when they didn't spank their misbehaving child hard enough—or if they spanked too hard.

Only one woman who had been trying for six years to have a baby became pregnant. Few people knew until the night, early in her pregnancy, she was carried to the hospital when it was feared she would lose the baby. The air was thick with animosity the next morning when her worried husband appeared at roll call. His face was gray.

TRANSFER TO BILIBID PRISON

AS THE DAYS WENT BY and the internees got hungrier and hungrier, they tacked magazine pictures of luscious baked hams, bowls of fresh fruit, and other delicious goodies on dormitory walls. Then they would stand before them and drool. At least in their imagination they were temporarily sated.

By December 1944, food was at a minimum while everything else was at a premium. Parents worked hard making little Christmas toys for their children from the odds and ends. Al made Katy a doll cradle out of bamboo for her birthday, and Nessie made her a small stuffed horse with material she cut from a red blanket.

Nessie had hoarded cassava flour so Katy might have a tiny cake on her birthday on December 11. She decorated it with five candles passed from mother to mother whenever a birthday was celebrated. She and Al had Dottie and the Morris children over for dinner. They dined on one of their precious tins of Spam. With the cake, they had "ice-cream" which Nessie made from soft rice, a bit of powdered milk, and a four-ounce tin of butter.

On Christmas Day, Al cut down a little pine tree from the hill above camp, and Nessie decorated it with a Santa Claus and two reindeer she made out of spools, cardboard, and bits of colored cloth. Katy was enchanted with it.

That evening, Nessie opened their last tin of Spam for dinner. She and Al invited Dottie for dinner. Afterwards, a young couple, Beth and John, joined them for dessert. Dottie had made a Christmas pudding out of rice and cornmeal, which she served with the sauce Beth had made from John's last cocoa, sugar, and powdered milk. Nessie popped *bucacao* to make popcorn balls (Katy had been given a quarter of a cup of *bucacao* for her birthday). They all thought they were in seventh heaven.

The next evening, the commandant assembled all the internees on the parade ground and announced they must be ready by dawn the next morning to be driven to Manila. There they would be interned in Bilibid Prison.

This decision was likely General Yamashita's. The "Tiger of Malaya" had arrived in the Philippines to take command of the Japanese forces just two weeks before General MacArthur landed on Leyte in October 1944. Knowing that the war was lost, Yamashita's strategy was to slow the American advance to Japan by mounting his defense of the Philippines in the mountains of northern Luzon. Clearly, he wanted the internees out of harm's way.[22]

Al and Nessie packed their few possessions, slept little, and in the chill darkness of early morning walked out to the parade grounds. There, trucks were lined up waiting to take

---

[22] Hastings, Max, *Retribution*, pp. 122, 223, 227.

them and the other internees to Bilibid. Thirty-seven internees and their most important belongings, plus five Japanese guards were assigned to each truck. Al was so busy helping the Sisters of St. Anne get safely stowed on their truck that for a moment Nessie was worried he wouldn't have time to hop on their truck. He jumped onto their truck so late that they were not able to sit together. During the journey down the tortuous Kennon Road to the central Luzon plain, and south from there to Manila, an exhausted old man beside Nessie rested his head on Nessie's shoulder while she held Katy in her lap.

The internees passed great numbers of vehicles heading north. Each was loaded with soldiers and equipment. Little did the internees realize they were witnessing the Japanese troop withdrawal into the mountains.

At the town of Binalonan, the convoy stopped for a badly needed rest. The guards marched all the women to a nearby Roman Catholic Church and bade them use it as a toilet. Most of the women did, but Nessie, Dottie, and Katy refused to desecrate the church and, regardless of the soldiers, squatted outside.

None of the internees was given food during the long trip. As they passed through one village, Al leaned over the side of the truck and bought a large bar of coconut candy from a villager. He shared it with Nessie, Katy, and Dottie.

Shortly after midnight, the convoy pulled into old Bilibid Prison in the heart of Manila. Before the war, it had housed the Philippines' worst criminals. The Japanese used it to incarcerate American soldiers. Before the Camp Holmes internees arrived, the Japanese moved the eight hundred soldiers into an adjacent, older section of the prison. Left behind were hundreds of filthy, bloodstained mattresses. Exhausted from the long day's drive, the Camp Holmes internees pushed the mattresses aside and slept on the floor or on wooden bed frames. Al was able to secure a bed frame for his, Nessie's, and Katy's use. It was made of boards about three inches wide spaced about the same distance apart. They had lost so much weight and become so thin, they could fit their pelvic bones in between the boards when they lay down to sleep.

The next morning, the internees all pitched in to clean the prison and to try to make it habitable. They scrubbed everything—floors, stairways, tables, chairs, and bed frames—and made huge bonfires of the mattresses. They covered the latrines in the front yard with gigantic mosquito nets to try to prevent the spread of dysentery, and they converted one of the wings of the prison into a small hospital. In the days and weeks that followed, they cleaned the hundred graves of American soldiers within the prison grounds.

LIBERATION

TWENTY-FOUR HOURS AFTER THEIR ARRIVAL at Bilibid, internees had their first meal. Henceforth, they were allotted only two meals a day, the first served at nine and the second at four. The meals consisted of wormy rice, sweet potatoes (while they lasted), and cornmeal full of weevils.

At Camp Holmes, the guards had made quite a show of weighing internees on a regular basis. After the move to Bilibid, they ceased to do so. When Al's weight fell below 110 and Nessie's below 100, they both stopped weighing themselves. They were starving to death.

Al continued to help in the kitchen as Alex's assistant, but Nessie was assigned a new job—cooking for camp members on outdoor stoves. A number of women shared the job, serving an hour or two several times a week. In the tropical heat, so unlike Baguio's temperate climate, the job was no joke. Nessie liked her new job except for an unfortunate incident. One day, when Nessie reported for work, the woman she was relieving told her which corn cake belonged to which woman, and which tin of "bread" belonged to which man. Then she added, "It won't be necessary to touch the pot of beans in the back. It won't be done for a couple of hours." Nessie left the beans alone and concentrated on the other culinary "delights." Fifteen minutes later a man came by for his pot of beans. He and two other men had pooled their last beans and Spam to celebrate a birthday.

"Why," Nessie said blithely, "they won't be done for a couple of hours yet."

"Oh," said the owner, "they're all cooked. They just needed to be heated."

They were heated up all right—charred black. Nessie almost wept as she stood there.

Shortly afterwards, Al came down with dengue fever. For a week, he ran a high fever, developed a rash, could keep little food down, and lost even more weight. He recovered, but was debilitated. Meanwhile, Nessie had ceased to menstruate and at times had such terrific cramps in her abdomen that she could not stand upright. Other women were in the same fix, and almost all the internees suffered from diarrhea. They could hardly make it to the toilets in time.

Fortunately for Al and Nessie, a camp doctor assigned them to the ground floor of the prison. They did not have the strength to walk up the incline to the second floor two or three times a day.

The prison was surrounded by thick, eighteen-foot-high cement walls, and the internees lived behind barred windows. Nevertheless, there were still things to see, including on one incredible day, an American plane. Internees cheered when they saw it fly above the city. A few days later Nessie watched a fight between an American plane and one of the enemy's. The American plane was hit and burst into flames seconds after the pilot bailed out. Her first reaction was how spectacular, how beautiful—until she realized what it really meant and was filled with horror.

Internees learned from their clandestine camp radio that General MacArthur's 37th Infantry had landed at Lingayen Gulf, to the north, on January 9, 1945, and that American troops were advancing on the city. At night, internees sat on steps in the prison and listened to the sounds of battle—big guns booming in the distance. From the flashes in the sky and the sound of the guns, they could estimate just how distant the American troops were. Never thinking of the death and destruction the big guns were causing, the internees found them comforting. They told each other they would be rescued soon. Their excitement and the heat made it difficult for them to sleep. Mothers would bathe their children, put them in their nightclothes, and then walk back and forth in the prison's courtyard, trying to get the children a little cooler and a little more tired so they, at least, could sleep.

After sweeping down the central Luzon plain, MacArthur's 37th Infantry met stiff resistance when it reached Manila. Retaking the city became one of "the ugliest battles of the Pacific War,"[23] and for a month, "the Sixth Army found itself committed to a street-by-street, often house-by-house struggle against suicidal Japanese

---

[23] Hastings, Max, *Retribution*, p. 231.

resistance."[24] The Japanese did not hesitate to kill Filipino civilians who got in their way, and many other civilians died under American gunfire.[25] Altogether, 1,000 American soldiers died in the battle, 16,665 Japanese, and 100,000 civilians.[26]

At dusk on February 3, Al was on the second floor visiting friends when he happened to gaze out the window and see something on the street below. He had no word for it. He had never seen a tank before. But he was sure it belonged to American troops, and he shouted, "They're here!"

The internees were afraid to show too much excitement, not wanting their Japanese guards to shoot them just before they were rescued. The guards had placed gasoline drums by the front gate and had wired the roof of the prison—with what the internees weren't sure.

Summoning all his strength, Al ran downstairs to Nessie and said, "Come upstairs and watch them come in!"

"No," Nessie replied, "now that they're here, I am going to bed and get some sleep."

She had been having difficulty sleeping for a long time. While almost everyone else sat up and talked all that night, she slept soundly.

But Bilibid was not liberated that night. Six hundred

---

[24] Ibid, p. 231
[25] Ibid, p. 237
[26] Ibid, p. 238

men of the First Cavalry, and the 37th Infantry had reached the Bilibid neighborhood, but they had only a few tanks with them. The tanks circled the neighborhood all night to give the Japanese a false impression of their strength.

Their strategy worked. The next morning the Japanese commandant and guards assembled the internees in the courtyard and announced they were being released. The officers quickly left the grounds, but the guards remained behind. Exuberant, the internees hoisted the American flag. They had sewn it in secret months before, and Nessie had embroidered the star for Oregon. But they had barely raised the flag when it was shot at. They quickly lowered it.

At sunset, the American soldiers drew close to Bilibid. As they approached, the Japanese guards came running through the prison with guns in hand to take up positions, but they held their fire. As the American soldiers drew even closer, the Japanese retreated to a far corner of the prison where they barricaded themselves in a small room. Their faces were ashen as they filed past the internees.

The American troops reached the gates of old Bilibid where the military prisoners were held. In answer to a query as to who was inside, an inmate cried out, "We're American prisoners of war."

"Prisoners of war, *hell*," came back the response. "*We're* here now!"

The troops knew there were military prisoners at Bilibid, but they were surprised to discover civilian internees also, particularly women and children. A young lieutenant was the first to enter the civilian section of the prison. The internees nearly mobbed him, their hearts bursting with joy, their faces streaming with tears.

To the internees he looked so big, so healthy, and so *good*. They spent the next hours just looking at him—at the amazing new helmet he wore, at his gun, at his boots. It didn't matter that it had been thirty-seven months since he himself had last seen the States. To them, he represented home!

Manila was a city burning. When the fire came within a few feet of Bilibid's front gates, the internees were evacuated. They took with them only blankets and a change of clothing. Women and small children were loaded onto trucks. Able-bodied women and men followed on foot until the trucks could return and pick them up.

As Al and Nessie waited to be evacuated, the military prisoners of war walked past them. Those prisoners were a pitiful sight, in rags, thin and bent over. Many were carried on stretchers, too weak to walk.

When it was their turn to leave, Al boosted Nessie and Katy onto the truck. One of the soldiers told Al to hop on also. He was grateful, as he was still weak from his bout of dengue fever, but he wasn't too happy when the truck passed some women walking.

The evacuees were driven to Ang Tibay, an enormous shoe factory outside city limits. American soldiers were quartered there, but they hastily removed their belongings so the evacuees could sleep in their places on the floor.

Once Al and Nessie were settled, Al went to see if there was anyone he knew among the military prisoners. He found Lieutenant Taulbee, whom he had last seen at Camp John Hay in Baguio almost two years before. The Lieutenant was hardly recognizable as the young man who had given Nessie a precious bar of soap in the Bontoc jail. He told Al that the Japanese had tortured him for three weeks.

The next morning, the evacuees were given their first taste of American Army food. They found the helpings so small, having hungered so long for huge plates of rice to fill their empty stomachs. They did not realize the food they had been given was more than most of them could consume—cereal with milk and sugar, dehydrated eggs, and hard biscuits with jam, plus good hot coffee. It more than satisfied them. In fact, Al and Nessie concluded that nothing they had ever eaten tasted quite so good.

The next morning they went for a short walk, with Katy in tow. Soldiers sitting in a Jeep nearby invited them to get in. They did—and they had such fun—not just talking, but also feeling as though they were going somewhere— although the Jeep didn't move an inch.

Then they did go somewhere—back to Bilibid that evening. The prison had escaped the fire, but it had been looted, completely stripped of everything the evacuees had left behind. Filipinos, doubtless thinking they had left for good—and with their own homes burning to the ground— found even the internees' pitiful belongings of value.

So the former internees started life afresh with the

clothes they had on their backs, one change of clothes, and the blankets they had taken with them to Ang Tibay.

Nessie wandered over to where the Sisters of St. Anne were camping to see how they were doing. The Mother Superior, never complaining herself, told her that two of the Sisters had been very uncomfortable the night before because they had been unable to take their blankets with them to Ang Tibay and now had none.

The Sisters had given Al and Nessie blankets shortly after their arrival at Camp Holmes. Now, without hesitation, Nessie returned the blankets to them. The Mother Superior gave Nessie a grateful smile and said, "Truly this is casting one's bread upon the waters."

The Japanese refused to surrender. They entrenched themselves in Manila's old walled city, and the American soldiers had to blow them to smithereens to get them out. Howitzers and machine guns continued to roar day after day and night after night. One lone Japanese plane dropped a bomb just outside Bilibid's walls, killing four American soldiers and wounding several others.

Once the walled city fell, the liberated internees were allowed to go outside the camp walls. Al persuaded Nessie and Dottie to join him on a walk to Santo Tomas to visit old friends who had been interned there. They were relieved to make it safely to Santo Tomas and back because there were still snipers in the area.

For the first time they noticed that Manila had been utterly destroyed in the fighting. The Filipino cook for the

American soldiers at Bilibid posted a sign by the mess that read, "The Japanese have made the Pearl of the Orient the Valley of Tears."

Soon, the internees had more food than they could eat. They found their daily ration of milk and sugar more than sufficient. In fact, there was enough sugar for Al to make candy, one of his favorite leisure-time pursuits before the war. His services were soon in demand, especially by young single women. Soldiers had begun to pay them quite a bit of attention. One or another of them would dash up to Al in the morning and ask, "Oh, Father, could you make me some fudge for this afternoon?"

Doctors gave each of the internees a physical exam. Army Intelligence interviewed Al and many others. Al had kept his involvement with the guerrillas secret from fellow internees, not wanting to jeopardize any of his guerrilla friends who had been captured or were still hiding out. He realized that it was important to establish a record of guerrilla activity in the Balbalasang region in order for village men who had served as guerrillas to receive back pay and benefits from the U.S. Army.

One afternoon, General MacArthur's wife visited Bilibid to meet the internees. The heat was intense, and Nessie happened to be lying on her bed dozing. She was aware of a woman dressed all in white walking by her bed and she thought in her dream-like state, "How remarkable!" Nessie considered the visit a gracious gesture, but some internees resented MacArthur's wife for coming into the prison so splendidly dressed.

There was also much excitement when an African-American soldier came into camp. Not only was he was the first African-American that most of the children had seen, but he also had a Jeep. He took the children for spins around the prison yard, to their great delight.

Another soldier, a Jewish boy from the Midwest, took a great interest in Katy. He took Al, Nessie, and Katy downtown where he insisted on buying Katy a pair of Filipina slippers and three lengths of dress material. He had a pet monkey, which he had acquired in the South Pacific and taught many tricks. The children followed him down the corridors whenever he came to call on Katy. He wanted to give her the monkey, but Al and Nessie declined the gift as graciously as they could.

Katy loved listing all the things she wanted when she reached the States: "Dresses and shoes (can I choose my own bedroom slippers?), a pair of pajamas—and we'll save all the tin cans for me to play with!"

REPATRIATION

AT THE END OF FEBRUARY, the never-to-be-forgotten-day came when the first internee was repatriated. No one even thought of being envious. They were just so glad that someone was at last going home.

Before their turn came, Al and Nessie received the sad news that both Garnett Morris and Walter Cushing's mining partner Pee Wee Ordun had perished. Desperate for factory labor, the Japanese had shipped thousands of military POWs to Japan, including Garnett and Pee Wee. Prisoners were kept in holds below deck to avoid aerial detection. They had no fresh air and were given little water or food. On December 13, 1944, the ship the two men were aboard was bombed and sunk by the U.S. Air Force in the Sea of Japan. Both men lost their lives, along with hundreds of other POWs.

In the first step of their repatriation, Al, Nessie, and Katy were flown to the island of Leyte in the central Philippines. Nessie and Katy were assigned to a beach camp where, with other women and children, they slept in big tents on mosquito-netted Army cots. They were grateful to be away from the bombing, strafing, and confusion of battle, and found the quiet wondrous. Al and the other men were housed at the town of Tacloban, not far away. The men walked over daily to be with their families and enjoyed sun bathing on the beach or taking a swim.

The soldiers gave a party for the children. Katy did not want to go as she was very shy, but Nessie insisted, knowing Katy would feel bad later when she heard reports about the party from the other children. Nessie took her to the waiting room where each child was matched with a soldier. Katy steadfastly refused to go to any of them until a great big burly fellow entered. He pointed at her and said, "There's my girl!" She ran, jumped into his arms, and sat in his lap to enjoy a delightful puppet show.

A week later, Al, Nessie, and Katy sailed home on the *Klipfontein*, a Dutch luxury liner that sailed into San Pablo Bay and moored just off Tacloban. Women with small children were assigned cabins with bathrooms. Nessie was most grateful that she and Katy were assigned their own cabin. Other women and older children were assigned bunks in large rooms. The men slept in the hold.

Nessie and Katy ate their breakfasts and dinners in one of the ship's large dining rooms. Nessie marveled at once again sitting at a table spread with white linen and set with silver. At breakfast, the women were given baskets of rolls and fancy breads, and platters of cheese and meat to make their lunches, which they ate on deck. Nessie made an extra sandwich for Al so he could join her and Katy for lunch and not have to stand in line for his own.

Their dinners were equally marvelous, especially the Dutch pastry for dessert. More than once, Nessie smuggled hers out of the dining room for Al or one of the wounded soldiers.

Before heading across the Pacific to San Francisco, the *Klipfontein* sailed to the Dutch East Indies, stopping at both Finch-haven and Biak. No one was allowed off ship, but soldiers came on board to meet the liberated POWs. At Biak, a soldier asked over the loudspeaker if there was anyone aboard from Massachusetts. Al was born and raised in Methuen, so up on deck he, Nessie, and Katy went to meet one of the biggest soldiers they had ever seen. He was an African-American. They had quite a visit, climaxed by his showing Al and Nessie the latest letter from his wife, on the last page of which she had imprinted a bright red lipstick kiss. As he left, he promised to come back in the afternoon.

True to his word, the soldier returned—but looking much heavier than he had that morning. After a careful glance around the deck, he pulled out of one pocket a carton of gum, which he handed to Katy, out of another came a carton of Hershey bars, which he gave to Nessie, and from under his shirt he pulled six bottles of beer for Al.

At last, the *Klipfontein* turned east and headed across the Pacific. On April 12, everyone was on deck in life jackets, waiting for muster and listening to the afternoon news broadcast when they learned of the death of President Roosevelt. They were stunned. Not a word was said. No one moved. Tears streamed down their faces, soldiers and civilians alike, men and women who had fought at Guadalcanal and Leyte, hidden in Luzon rainforests, and come close to starving in concentration camps. It was as though their father was suddenly gone without warning. Franklin Delano Roosevelt had stood for everything America meant to them—all its goodness and all its strength.

On a glorious spring day, the *Klipfontein* sailed through the Golden Gate. When Al and Nessie disembarked in San Francisco, they were given POW cards and ration books. Their plan was to take a train to Portland, Oregon, and then spend time recuperating in a small town on the coast where Nessie's father had retired during the war. The earliest tickets they could get were for Monday, so they were put up at the St. Francis Hotel for the weekend. Dressed in clothes they were issued after their rescue at Bilibid, they looked a sight. Al was in Army clothes, and Nessie wore a WAC shirt and skirt and a WAVE coat. Katy had been given a pretty blue wool dress when they disembarked. Of the three, she was the most fashionable.

When eating dinner at a restaurant that evening, Nessie ordered a baked potato for Katy. When it was placed in front of her, she remarked, "Mommy, don't they have butter in this country either?"

A gentleman sitting nearby overheard her. He got up, crossed to their table, and handed Nessie a small brown paper sack, saying, "Perhaps you would like this."

It was a quarter-pound of butter. Nessie was grateful and appreciated his gift even more later, when she became familiar with ration books and realized how generous the man had been.

When they got to Portland, Al and Nessie purchased new wardrobes for themselves and Katy, met with reporters from the *Oregonian* and the *New York Herald Tribune*, who interviewed them about their experiences, then slipped away with Nessie's father to their retreat in Nelscott by the Pacific Ocean.

Townsfolk asked Al and Nessie no questions about the war, requested no lectures, and hardly spoke except to pass the time of day. Months later, Nessie learned that her father had asked the townsfolk not to bother them. Al and Nessie were most grateful. After their years of internment, they needed quiet and time to be alone.

SERVICE des PRISONNIERS de GUERRE
俘虜郵便

NAME ___ERNESTINE C. GRIFFITHS_____

NATIONALITY ___AMERICAN_____

PHILIPPINE INTERNMENT CAMP NO. __3__ .

檢閱濟
比島軍抑留所
U.S. CENSOR 12749

TO: ___DR. CHARLES E. COLES_____

___NELSCOTT, OREGON_____

___U.S.A.___

June 30, 1944

IMPERIAL JAPANESE ARMY

1. I am interned at Philippine Internment Camp No. __3__

2. My health is — excellent; good; fair; poor.

3. Message. (Limited to 25 words.) ALL WELL. KATHARINE IN

KINDERGARTEN NOW AND LOVES IT. OUR GARDEN WONDERFUL

HELP WITH TOMATOES, POTATOES, CORN. STILL HOPING FOR

A LETTER. LOVE TO ALL.

ERNESTINE C. GRIFFITHS
Signature

In 1944, the Japanese allowed internees to send postcards to relatives in the United States. Because the mail was censored, Nessie chose her words carefully when she wrote to her father in Oregon.

RETURN TO BALBALASANG

WITHIN A YEAR OF HIS REPATRIATION, Al returned to the Philippines, six weeks before I was born in May 1946, just two months before the Philippines gained its independence from the United States. Nessie followed a year later with Katy and me. She waited until Al had the opportunity to rebuild St. Paul's Mission. Dottie also returned to the Philippines after recovering at her home in England.

Prior to his return, Al worked tirelessly in Oregon to accumulate boxes and boxes of clothing, medical supplies, food, and seeds for Balbalasang villagers. He requested donations from relief agencies, churches, relatives, and friends.

From Balbalasang, Al wrote Nessie that he was busy rebuilding the mission and helping villagers with their war damage claims. Sadly, he reported that Chief Puyao was bedridden and not expected to live. The Chief had surrendered not long after Al and Nessie were interned. The Japanese had summoned him to Lubuagan, and on the way, he suffered a crippling stroke.

But Chief Puyao was stronger than anyone realized and he lived two and a half more years. At the Chief's request, Al founded St. Paul's Memorial High School, built on a hillside next to the church plaza. The school memorialized three Balbalasang men who died in combat during the war.

Frederick Dao-ayan served as the headmaster, and Nessie taught a few English classes.

Faculty and students at St. Paul's Memorial High School, with Principal Frederick Dao-ayan and English teacher Nessie Griffiths at left.

Great was the mourning, and great the celebration of his life when Chief Puyao died on November 2, 1949. In accordance with Tingguian custom, his body was bathed, dressed, and seated in an armchair on a bamboo platform in the main room of his home. His feet rested on an ancient Chinese jar embossed with dragons. Strands of agate and gold draped from his head. In his lap were five Chinese plates. In the top plate was a pack of his favorite cigarettes—Lucky Strikes—plus a box of matches. At his right were two Spanish mahogany canes, each crested in silver, and a Japanese samurai sword. A wreath of marigold, bougainvillea, and calla lilies hung from the ceiling above his head, the lilies forming a cross. Displayed on the back wall were red Tingguian horse blankets and two of the Chief's most prized possessions—an American flag, and a blue naval officer's coat given to him by William Howard Taft when Taft served as Governor General of the Philippines. To his left, piled from floor to ceiling against the wall were bundles of *palay*, evidence of his great wealth.

Visitors from throughout Kalinga and beyond arrived to pay their respects. With the help of neighbors and friends, Chief Puyao's family butchered and roasted pigs and carabaos, and cooked huge quantities of rice to feed their many guests. At his wife's request, Al held vespers every evening at the Chief's house. Afterward, villagers and visitors entertained themselves throughout the night, drinking *basi*, singing, dancing—and challenging each other to games of physical endurance.

Chief Puyao's funeral was held the fourth day after his death. The *Padji* conducted the service at St. Paul's Church, which the Chief had been instrumental in bringing to his people. The Chief was accorded full Philippine military honors because he had served as a military advisor to the guerrillas. His coffin was draped with a Philippine flag. As former guerrillas carried the coffin from Puyao's house to the church, Philippine Constabulary soldiers fired a volley in his honor. The *Padji* and Rev. Theodore Saboy, a Balbalasang villager ordained to the Episcopal priesthood, led the procession, followed by the coffin bearers, the Chief's family and close relatives, Boy Scout troops, villagers and guests, and, lastly, the Chief's saddled but riderless horse. The church filled to overflowing.

Chief Puyao had asked to be buried at the site of his former home, which Captain Hirano had burned to the ground. His sandy grave was lined with Saltan River stones. As his coffin was lowered into the grave, the Constabulary fired a final salute to this last great Tingguian chief. He had led his people ably in peace and war.

Balbalasang men beating gansas at Chief Puyao's funeral feast.

Chief Puyao's funeral feast.

Chief Puyao's grave.

AFTERWORD

MY FATHER WROTE HIS ACCOUNT of his wartime experiences aboard the ship that took him back to the Philippines in 1946. His narrative focuses on his guerrilla activity and the months he and his family spent hiding from the Japanese in the forests of northern Luzon. It ends with their internment in Camp Holmes in April 1943. My mother wrote her account in the early 1950s after we left the Philippines for what we thought was the last time. Her description of the months they spent hiding from the Japanese relied heavily on my father's account. Her narrative also includes the months they spent in prison camp, their liberation, and their repatriation. And it describes the three years my family spent in Balbalasang after the war—from 1947 to 1950.

My mother wrote her account because she wanted Katy and me to have a record of their wartime experiences, and of our life in Balbalasang after the war, only a bit of which I've drawn on here. When she completed her manuscript, I suspect she wondered when Katy or I would ask to read it.

I made the first request. Being the youngest member of the family, I wanted to know what I had missed. Whenever my parents met someone they had known in prison camp they always introduced me as their "postwar addition"—the only member of the family not to have shared in their benchmark experience. One day when I was in the fifth grade and home from school sick, I asked to read the manuscript. Mother quickly assented. I was eleven years old and found the story to be a great adventure, full of suspense and drama made even more exciting by the fact that I knew all the characters and was even mentioned myself.

But the pain and difficulty of the war years for my parents were not as apparent to me then as they are now. The fact that they almost never discussed their wartime experiences when I was growing up—rarely even in the company of friends who had been in prison camp with them—made me realize that the war had left a very deep mark on their lives.

Every now and then, I would wake at night to hear my father shouting in his sleep. Mother would explain the next morning that he had a recurrent nightmare about the war— of Japanese soldiers with bayonets drawn, chasing him through the forest. Years later, after my parents retired, the rector of the local Episcopal church asked my father to give a talk about his wartime experiences. He agreed, but shortly after he started his presentation, he was so overcome with emotion that he could not continue. This behavior was not characteristic, and surely it surprised and embarrassed him.

My mother did not suffer from nightmares, but she struck me at times as a very anxious woman, worried about matters that wouldn't concern the rest of us. I often asked myself, "Why is she worried about *that*? She survived the war, *didn't she?*"

Steve and Katy Griffiths on the banks of the Saltan River, circa 1948.

Al and Nessie Griffiths in Balbalasang, circa 1948.

Perhaps surviving life-threatening challenges does not give you more strength, but may, in an insidious way, sap your remaining confidence. During the war, however, there is no doubt my mother was very brave, supporting my father and sheltering my sister in one crisis after another.

In the introduction to his account of the war, my father writes:

> I never thought my adventures rather unusual. Many Americans went through the same kind of hardships, lost as much weight, and were as glad to see the American troops arriving as I was. Perhaps, however, my experience was a little more unique than most of my fellow missionaries since I, together with my family and Miss Taverner, refused to surrender to the

Japanese and were finally hunted down and captured. We were amongst the last of the Americans to be rounded up and finally interned.

My parents' wartime experiences were different than those of other civilian POWs in the Philippines. Their experiences—and their ultimate survival—were shaped by very unusual circumstances. First was Balbalasang's extreme isolation. News was slow to reach the village, and mail often went missing. As a consequence, my father never received the letter from his Bishop telling him not to get involved with the guerrillas. If he had received it, there is no doubt he would have complied. He, Nessie, and Dottie would have surrendered to the Japanese at the first opportunity, no matter how strongly Chief Puyao and the Balbalasang people would have urged him not to. My father was obliged to obey his Bishop.

Second, my father was a Chaplain in the U.S. Army Reserve, and that complicated matters. He viewed his participation in the guerrilla movement as a natural extension of this role. As a chaplain, he was a non-combatant. Nevertheless, he chose to participate in the ambush at Lamonan. Ironically, the nighttime ambush was over by the time he got there. At Cushing's orders, he had spent the day making sure all villagers had evacuated Balbalasang and that his family, Garnett's wife and children, and Dottie were safe at their hiding place at Mapga.

Third, the dynamic guerrilla leader Walter Cushing

operated a mine not far from Balbalasang. He was a neighbor of sorts and had visited my parents before the war, striking up a friendship. He charmed them, and my father did not hesitate to support Cushing's decision to establish a guerrilla unit. My parents always viewed Cushing as a genuine war hero.

Fourth, my father and the mission nurse, Dottie Taverner, were very well liked and respected by Chief Puyao and the Balbalasang people. My father spoke the Tingguian dialect, and he was friendly and outgoing. He hiked throughout the region to mission stations served by St. Paul's Mission in Balbalasang, getting to know many more people than just the villagers of Balbalasang. At her dispensary, the skilled nurse, Dottie, and her assistant, Anne Duñgo, treated hundreds and hundreds of patients each year. Throughout the war, Chief Puyao and the Balbalasang people took great personal risks to hide and feed my parents and sister and Dottie—a true measure of their devotion to them.

Fifth—and perhaps most significantly—Chief Puyao was sharp, strong-willed, and unstintingly loyal to America. His support of the guerrilla movement was steadfast. He consistently urged my father not to surrender, and refused to surrender himself even when the Japanese took members of his family hostage. Furthermore, he was a very shrewd judge of character and the first to suspect that the lowlander Concepcion was a spy for the Japanese.

Sixth, Japanese soldiers found my sister Katy a delight.

She reminded them of the infant children and siblings they had left behind. They went out of their way to give her treats and extra food. Her presence helped personalize the relationship between captor and captive and may have been key to the Japanese placing my father in a civilian internment camp, rather than a military camp. If he had been placed in a military camp, as Garnett Morris was, it is likely he would not have survived the war.

Seventh, Colonel Watanabe, who condemned my father to death at his headquarters in Bontoc, was a Christian, a rarity among Japanese military officers.[27] My father was not aware of this fact (and I only learned of it recently). I will always wonder if their shared faith contributed to Watanabe's decision not to execute him. We'll never know, but Watanabe's religious faith adds irony to his encounter with my father. He gave my father the royal chewing out he expected to receive from his Bishop for getting involved with the guerrillas.

Perhaps a more compelling factor in Watanabe's decision not to execute my father was his awareness—based on Concepcion's report—that the *Padji* was well regarded by Chief Puyao and the Tingguian people. Executing him would have angered them greatly, further stalling the Japanese goal of pacification.

After leaving the Philippines in 1950, my family moved to Kirkland, Washington, where my father was in charge of

---

[27] Norling, Bernard, *Intrepid Guerrillas of North Luzon*, p. 89.

two Episcopal churches. He did an outstanding job serving both, but he missed the Philippines, so it was no surprise when he accepted an offer in 1954 to become the headmaster of Brent School in Baguio. He had served as the chaplain at Brent when he first went to the Philippines in 1931.

I have no doubt that one of the reasons my father accepted the position was that it would give us an opportunity to visit Balbalasang. We did so for a few days every summer. Those trips are among the most precious memories of my childhood. I loved the adventure of hiking to the village through a tropical rainforest, and my parents enjoyed visiting their friends and St. Paul's Mission, now served by a Filipino priest. Every day we swam in the cold and turbulent waters of the Saltan River, still as fresh and sparkling as champagne. We would shoot the rapids, then stretch out on sun-baked boulders to warm up. Often, on our last evening in the village, a dance would be held in our honor. My father would lead everyone in singing a few favorite songs, and we would dance to the beat of *gansas* around a huge bonfire and sip *basi* from a glass passed hand-to-hand around the circle.

My parents visited Balbalasang for the last time in the spring of 1968, just weeks before they retired. My father had been invited to give the commencement address at St. Paul's Memorial High School, which he had founded after the war. He took great pleasure in the success of the school and the Balbalasang mission, which continued to thrive.

My parents retired to the same coastal town in Oregon where they had sought refuge after the war. They built a house on a hill with a view of the Pacific Ocean through a strand of western hemlock and Sitka spruce. Each of the rooms glowed with artifacts from the Philippines, most of them gifts from Balbalasang villagers: ancient Chinese jars, head axes, spears, *pasikings*, and baskets.

But what they both liked best about their new home was the sound of the distant, thunderous surf. It reminded them, they said, of the Saltan River, evoking memories of the years they had fallen asleep to the roar of the river—and breathed the scent of orange blossoms mixed with pine.

BIBLIOGRAPHY

Cogan, Frances B., *Captured: The Japanese Internment of American Civilians in the Philippines 1941-45*, University of Georgia Press, Athens and London, 2000.

Concepcion, Report to Colonel Nakashima, 1942.

Crouter, Natalie, *Forbidden Diary*, edited with an Introduction by Lynn Z. Bloom, Burt, Franklin & Company, New York, 1980.

Death, Escape & Liberation: POWs in the Philippines During World War II. Julian, California, Traditions Military Videos, DVD, 2005.

Fry, Howard T., *A History of the Mountain Province*, revised edition, New Day Publishers, Quezon City, 2006.

Griffiths, Alfred L., *For God and Country*, unpublished manuscript, 1946.

Griffiths, Ernestine Coles, *Mrs. Padji*, unpublished manuscript, 1953.

Hastings, Max, *Retribution*, Alfred A Knopf, New York, 2008.

Norling, Bernard, *The Intrepid Guerrillas of North Luzon*, The University Press of Kentucky, Lexington, Kentucky, 1999.

Ordun, M.B., *Walter M. Cushing Guerrilla Leader and Hero of the Ilocos Provinces*, unpublished manuscript, Cabanatuan Prison

Camp No. 1, May 22, 1943.

Worcester, Dean C., *The Philippines Past and Present*, Volume II, The MacMillan Company, Norwood Press, 1914.

ACKNOWLEDGMENTS

MANY THANKS TO ALL MY RELATIVES and friends who have read various versions of this manuscript over the years. Special thanks to members of my writing group in Lincoln City, Oregon, who offered me advice and support and patiently listened to me read excerpts from the final version of the manuscript. They are Ron Lovell, Libby Durbin, Vickie Meneses, Pat Ferguson, Carole Carr, and the late Wilma Rogers. Thanks also to Kristina Burbank for encouraging us to form the group. I owe you all a debt of gratitude.

Much appreciation also goes to Julie Fiedler for her edits and for preparing the maps, and to Delfin Tolentino of the University of the Philippines in Baguio for his sage editorial advice.

About the Author

STEPHEN GRIFFITHS earned a B. A. in English from Hobart College and a Ph.D. in Anthropology from the University of Hawaii. He is the author of *Emigrants, Entrepreneurs, and Evil Spirits: Life in a Philippine Village*, published by the University of Hawaii Press. After a 30-year career with the Sierra Club, Griffiths retired in 2009. He lives in Lincoln City on the Oregon coast.

INDEX

Jones, Isabella Province, 77
Juan, 89, 90

Kalinga, 14, 15, 25, 55, 62, 77,
    104, 107, 132, 159
Kalinga Academy, 46, 49, 63,
    104
Klipfontein, 152-154

Laganilang, 14, 23
Lamonan, 49-55, 65, 106, 167
Leyte, 138, 151, 153
Lingayen Gulf, 38, 143
Los Baños, 62
Lubuagan, 14, 25, 33, 46, 49-50,
    54, 55, 59, 61, 64, 65, 72, 83,
    89, 103, 104, 129, 157
Luzon, 11, 13, 15, 23, 35, 41, 46,
    82, 138-143, 153, 163, 169

Maatop, 52, 72, 73, 79, 80, 82,
    83, 97, 104, 110, 111
MacArthur, General, 61, 83,
    138, 143, 149
Manila, 11, 17, 23, 28, 32, 35,
    45, 107, 138, 139, 143, 146,
    148
Manila Bay, 31
Manuel, 74-76
Mapga, 47, 51-65, 167
Mapga River, 46, 51
Marcus, 85, 87-91, 97

Martinez, 68
Masablang, 63-65, 70, 72
Maymaya, 30, 50
McKim, Nellie, 117
Meratio, Sergeant, 104, 111
Morris family, 40, 41, 43, 44,
    47, 51, 52, 56, 58, 59, 63, 74,
    76, 79, 80, 82, 97, 132, 167
Morris, Garnett, 50, 53, 55,
    151, 169
Mountain Province, 33, 45, 100
Mt. Data Rest House, 49

Nagel, Rev., 46, 49, 63
New York Herald Tribune, 155

Ordun, Pee Wee, 32, 41-44, 54,
    151
Oregonian, 155
Oura, Major, 128

Pantikian, 102
Pasil River, 103, 104
Peabody, Rev. Malcolm, 13
Pearl Harbor, 130
Perryam, Captain, 82, 111-114
Philippine Constabulary, 73,
    74, 77, 97, 102, 112, 160
President Hoover, 32

Rainbow Mine, 32
Red Cross, 121-123, 127